Some Essential Features
of Nkrumaism

Some Essential Features of Nkrumaism

By Panaf Books
and the
Editors of
"The Spark"

Panaf
London

Some Essential Features of Nkrumaism

First published 1964
Reprinted 1970, 1975

© Copyright Panaf Books 2002

All rights reserved. No part of this publication may be reproduced, stored in retrieval system, or transmitted, in any form or by any means, electronic, mechanical, photocopying, recording or otherwise, without the prior permission in writing of Panaf Books, nor be otherwise circulated in any form of binding or cover other than that in which it is published, nor without a similar condition including this condition being imposed on subsequent purchaser.

ISBN 0 901787 1 59

PANAF BOOKS

75 Weston Street
London SE1 3RS (UK)

Printed in Great Britain
by Antony Rowe Ltd, Eastbourne

PUBLISHER'S NOTE

Since the first publication of *Some Essential Features of Nkrumaism* in 1964, further works of Kwame Nkrumah have been published. These are *Neocolonialism: The last stage of imperialism, Challenge of the Congo, Axioms, Dark Days in Ghana, Handbook of Revolutionary Warfare, Class Struggle in Africa, Revolutionary Path* and *The Struggle Continues.* In addition, there has been a revised edition of *Consciencism* which was made necessary because, in the words of the author: "the African Revolution has decisively entered a new phase, the phase of armed struggle", and the succession of military coups "have brought into sharp relief the nature and the extent of the class struggle in Africa".

Part One of this book consisting of Foreword and chapters one to six inclusive is the original text of *Some Essential Features of Nkrumaism* by editors of *The Spark*. Part Two, containing chapters, seven, eight and nine, by editors of Panaf Books, are published for the first time. They deal with the works of Nkrumah after 1964 and particularly with the very important post-coup period spent in Conakry, Guinea.

The consistency and continuity of Nkrumah's political thought and the development of his ideas shown in this summary of some of the fundamental principles and programme of Nkrumaism, provides basic material for the study of current socialist revolutionary change in Africa.

CONTENTS

PART ONE

Foreword — 11

1. The fight against colonialism — 15
2. Consolidation of people's power — 32
3. Socialist development — 50
4. African unity — 70
5. The party — 85
6. The philosophy of our revolution — 102

PART TWO

Introduction — 129

7. Neocolonialism — 133
8. Class struggle and the armed phase of the African Revolution — 145
9. Socialist All-African Union Government — 157

SOME ESSENTIAL FEATURES
OF NKRUMAISM

Foreword

With the publication of *Consciencism*,* Dr. Kwame Nkrumah adds to an already impressive volume of work which provides guidance and inspiration to all those working for the liberation of Africa in different countries at varying levels of struggle.

This handbook of some aspects of the teachings of Kwame Nkrumah, based on a series of articles in *The Spark*, provides a comprehensive survey of his outstanding works, *Towards Colonial Freedom*, *Africa Must Unite* and *Consciencism*.

Here we have a lucid outline of the main principles, experiences and per-

---

*Consciencism: Philosophy and Ideology for Decolonization, by Kwame Nkrumah, (Paperback) Panaf Books, 1970.

spectives which have inspired Dr. Kwame Nkrumah and the Convention People's Party in the successful struggles for independence and in the present task of consolidating political power and laying the foundations for a socialist Ghana through national reconstruction.

It is a measure of Dr. Nkrumah's farsightedness and profound intellectual grasp of scientific revolutionary theory that he has never confined himself to the solving of Ghana's problems alone. He has constantly explained that independence can be guaranteed ultimately only by the unity of all African states. Here we have the essence of his theory of African unity with practical proposals for its realization.

This book is a necessity for any student of African problems. But above all it is vitally necessary for all those who seek to play their part in the African revolution. It is their handbook of positive action.

Basing himself on the Marxist analysis of imperialism and its theories of social change, Dr. Nkrumah applies these principles to the successive stages of the struggle for Ghana's freedom. All the time he draws lessons from actual practical experiences, thus continuously enriching the ideology on which the program for the present and future are based.

This book is divided into six chapters. The first chapter deals with the nature of imperialism, the inevitability of opposition to it and how the struggle should be organized. Chapter two explains what political power is and how the newly independent African country must transform the state inherited from colonialism and develop new constitutions and political forms; the third chapter outlines the various stages from national economic reconstruction to the building of socialism, and is followed in chapter four by the definition of the role of the party and how it is organized. The final chapter outlines the philosophical basis of the African revolution.

Simply, yet without vulgarization, the

essential features of Nkrumaism are set out. For those who have already personally experienced some of the struggles of the African revolution, the book will serve as a reminder of the vital lessons which they need to carry with them in struggles still remaining. To others and especially to young people, coming to revolutionary political ideas for the first time, this book will be a revelation of the power of scientific revolutionary theory. It will be an inspiration to them to deepen their studies and to join the ranks of those already taking positive action in the fight for Africa's liberation.

THE EDITOR

PART ONE

CHAPTER ONE

The Fight against Colonialism

Kwame Nkrumah is a revolutionary. He made his debut in politics in the mid-'forties when the revolutionary ferment in world history hit an all-time high—a period characterized by the general weakening of imperialism coupled with the rise of U.S. imperialism to the position of preeminence among the imperialist powers, the emergence of the world socialist system, the victorious sweep of national liberation in Asia, the awakening of Africa and the birth of the U.N. as an instrument capable of exerting a moral force in international affairs. He entered the arena and lives in a revolutionary era.

Quite naturally his ideas have grown and crystallized within that context.

But Kwame Nkrumah is not an ordinary revolutionary. He has been buoyed up by the revolutionary ideas of his age; but to the store of revolutionary knowledge and experience he has made significant contributions. In Africa's struggle to liquidate colonialism in all its forms and to build a socialist society Kwame Nkrumah is both an architect and an engineer, a seer and a leader, a thinker and a builder.

From the very beginning Kwame Nkrumah has had an all-Africa perspective. However, he was forced by the naked facts of African political life to start his activities as a leader of the people in his own home country—Ghana (then Gold Coast). Accordingly, Nkrumah's teachings could be divided into two closely related categories: the struggle within a single African country and the struggle on the all-African plane. In the first category he deals with the national revolution, the problems of consolidating and democratizing political power in the newly emergent African state, and the problem of economic and social reconstruction leading to a socialist society.

Under the second category, Kwame Nkrumah treats the problem of linking the politically independent African states with the struggle for the liquidation of colonialism (with its variant apartheid) and neo-colonialism throughout Africa.

While in the first category he deals with problems of the national, the democratic and the socialist revolutions, in the second, he deals with the African revolution.

Between 1945 and 1947 Kwame Nkrumah was a student in London (at the London School of Economics and Political Science). He took an active part in the politics of the colored and colonial peoples. He quickly identified himself with the Pan-African Congress, an organization concerned with the rights of African people and their struggle against colonialism. But he succeeded in giving that organization a much needed orientation. For his contact with the Pan-African Congress contributed greatly to that organization going a step further in its activities— from a mere critique of colonial oppression to the drawing up of a formula of action aimed at overthrowing colonial rule. This fighting formula was adopted at the Pan-African Congress held in Manchester, England, October 15–21, 1945, as a *Declaration to the Colonial Peoples of the World*. It was written by Kwame Nkrumah.

Nkrumah's next big effort came in 1947, when he reduced his ideas on the nature of imperialism and how to fight it into a book which has now been published under the title *Towards Colonial Freedom*. This book, now a classic of the African struggle, contains all Nkrumah's ideas about how to organize and lead the national liberation movement in the fight for the overthrow of colonialism and for building in its place a new society "in which the free development of each is the condition for the free development of all." The rest of this chapter is based wholly on this book because in Nkrumah's own words it "is exactly as it was written originally" and "the views I expressed then are precisely the views I hold today" (*Foreword*, p. x).

Nkrumah rejects outright the notion that the aim of imperialism is to bring civilization to a people (doctrine of "assimilation") or to prepare them for self-rule (doctrine of "trusteeship" or "partnership"). Imperialism, he asserts, is a doctrine of exploitation. In terms of government, it "is the policy which aims at creating, organizing and maintaining an empire" (p. 1). Contemporary imperialism is the dominance of finance capital. It supersedes the dominance of industrial capital which was preceded historically by the dominance of merchant capital.

Nkrumah then accepts the teachings of Marx and Lenin which he describes as "the most searching and penetrating analysis of economic imperialism" (p. 11). Imperialism is not just an accident. It is a logical outcome of the inner contradictions of the capitalist system and its own inconsistencies "foreshadow its doom and demolition" (p. 11).

Colonialism is characterized by the following features:

(1) the export of capital to sources of raw materials;

(2) the frenzied struggle for monopolistic control of these sources of raw materials;

(3) exclusive markets for manufactured goods of the imperialist powers;

(4) making colonial peoples non-manufacturing dependencies and prohibiting them from trading with other nations except the "mother country";

(5) exploitation of colonial cheap labor. "The purpose of this exploitation and oppression is to squeeze out super-profits" (p. 39).

Thus colonialism is something practiced not by a nation as a whole but by some financial interests and monopoly groups within the nation primarily for their own good.

Note that some of the spoils of colonialism are passed on to the government of the "home country" in the form of taxes, and to a privileged section of workers in the "home country" in the form of higher wages on which an "aristocracy of labor" is reared.

However, it is these financial groups and monopoly combines that exercise control and direction over the colonial governments. Summarizing, Nkrumah writes: "The colonies are thus a source of raw materials and cheap labor, a dumping ground for spurious surplus goods to be sold at exorbitant prices. Therefore, these colonies become avenues for capital investment, *not for the benefit and development of the colonial peoples, but for the benefit of the investors, whose agents are the governments concerned*" (p. xvii).

Imperialism, in its operation and very nature, creates the conditions for its own destruction. In the colonies, it helps the "emergence of a colonial intelligentsia" which plays a big part in "the awakening of national consciousness among colonial peoples." It also leads inevitably to "the emergence of a working class movement" for capitalist exploitation must of necessity bring into being a class of workers. And these three elements, fused together, lead to "the growth of a national liberation movement" (p. 39).

In the "mother country," imperialism leads to increased conflict among capitalist and financial groups. In addition, the development of capitalism to an advanced stage brings into being a large and powerful "proletarian movement in the capitalist countries" (p. 41). This movement also has an interest in the destruction of capitalism and *ipso facto* imperialism.

Between the imperialist countries themselves, imperialism means a "struggle for a redivision of the already divided world, a struggle waged with particular fury by new financial groups and powers seeking newer territories and colonies against the old groups and powers which cling tightly to that which they have grabbed" (pp. 38–39). This struggle often leads to wars, both local and global.

Thus the national liberation movement in the colonies and the proletarian movement in the imperialist countries gradually and inevitably reinforce each other and thus constitute "a coalition ... against the world front of imperialism" (p. 41).

Having traced the genesis and shown the inevitability of the national liberation movement as well as its world relations with other powerful forces fighting imperialism and its creator capitalism, the next problem for Nkrumah is how to organize the colonial struggle.

The first thing he says is, "Organization of the Colonial Masses." It must be "an organization of labor and youth" (p. 41). And it must seek to abolish political illiteracy, that is, bring political education to the entire people.

Nkrumah's teachings on the nature, the composition and the leadership of this "organization of the colonial masses" are extremely important and constitute the kernel of his political faith. Knowing full well that African society is riddled with economic interests, social groupings and class interests, Nkrumah insists that the "organization must root itself and secure its basis and strength in the labor movement, the farmers (the workers and peasantry) and the youth" (pp. 41–42).

It does not specifically exclude any group or class in a position to join or contribute towards the fight against colonialism. But it makes it very clear that "the organized force of labor, the organized farmers and the responsible and cogent organization of youths" constitute "the motive force of the colonial liberation movement" (p. 42). Even in his appeal to "farmers" Nkrumah is careful to make a vital distinction, for at p. 41 he regards farmers as "workers and peasantry," in other words the rural workers and the small (self-employed) farmers.

Again, in the 1945 Pan-African Congress *Declaration to the Colonial Peoples of the World,* written by Nkrumah and attached as appendix to *Towards Colonial Freedom,* the leadership of the workers in the colonial struggle is emphasized. The relevant portion reads: "Colonial workers must be in the front lines of the battle against imperialism" (p. 45).

At the time he wrote (1947) Nkrumah knew what harm intellectualism had done to the colonial struggle. It had retarded its speed and diluted its radical content. He also foresaw, with real prophetic insight, the betrayal of the national liberation movement through opportunism which more often than not arises from the intellectual and aspiring business classes. The role of the intellectuals, Nkrumah insists, is to clear the way for the upsurge of a powerful labor movement by "fighting for trade union rights, the right to form cooperatives, freedom of the press, assembly, demonstration and strike; freedom to print and read the literature which is necessary for the education of the masses" (p. 45). Admittedly, this is the task for which intellectuals as a rule are admirably fitted. He goes further to counsel that "the type of education" given to the national liberation movement "should do away with that kind of intelligentsia who have become the very architects of colonial enslavement" (p. 41).

Nkrumah's teachings on the position of workers and toiling masses generally in the national liberation movement cannot be overstressed. For it is precisely a glossing over of this point or a confused understanding of it that often leads to tragedy—to the not uncommon experience of the national liberation movement losing its bearings or failing to achieve all its objectives.

Briefly stated, the correct application of Nkrumah's view insures two things. In the first place it insures that the national liberation movement moves on swiftly from the termination of colonial rule to the building of a socialist society. If the working people are not in the "front lines," the probability is strong that after political independence a capitalist (and therefore, neo-colonialist) regime will be erected instead of the socialist society envisaged by the people.

In the second place, only an organization based on the revolutionary initiative of the masses has the staying power which is so essential in the fight against an enemy whose principal weapons are intrigues, subterfuges, inducements and delay used in conjunction with bullets and bayonets. It alone will guarantee success should a resort to "positive action" be forced on the national liberation movement.

Again, it is a tribute to his analytical insight that at a time when some colonial politicians either ignored the masses whom they contemptuously refer to as the "rabble" or merely used the masses to play their game of saber rattling which formed part of the war of nerves against imperialism, Nkrumah boldly recognized the existence of classes in African society and entrusted the dynamic role in the struggle for freedom and socialism to the most revolutionary of these classes—the workers, peasants and youth.

Nkrumah sees the national liberation movement as achieving its objectives in three interlocked stages. The first stage is the struggle for freedom from colonial rule. The key to victory in this stage is the conquest of political power. Hence his famous dictum "Seek ye first the political kingdom."

As soon as political independence is won, the first stage closes and the second opens. This second stage is concerned with the creation of a political system in which power is wielded by the people themselves and not by a class of men who think they know best what is good for the people. It is during this stage that the newly-won political power is consolidated and rendered safe from the intrigues and machinations of imperialism which is always seeking for new ways and forms to re-establish itself. The fight is for "democratic freedom" which Nkrumah defines as "the establishment of a democracy in which sovereignty is vested in the broad masses of the people" (p. 43).

It must be added that success at stage two is a necessary and indispensable condition for proceeding to stage three. This is the stage when the struggle is for the total reconstruction of society, when a new and just society is built in place of the oppressive and exploitative one created by colonialism. The basic task here is "freedom from poverty and economic exploitation." This of course means the abolition of capitalism as an economic system and the substitution of socialism in its place.

Thus the national liberation movement moves through three stages to achieve its objectives of freedom from colonial rule, people's political power and socialism. In the words of Nkrumah, "goal of the national liberation movement is the realization of complete and unconditional independence and the building of a society of peoples in which the free development of each is the condition for the free development of all" (p. 43).

Lastly, positive action. To a great extent Nkrumah is known to the African masses as the father of "positive action." Some political critics think this was merely imposed on Nkrumah in 1950 by the exigencies of the Gold Coast struggle. This assessment is incorrect. Nkrumah is not a pragmatist. On the contrary, he is a leader who charts and sees his way long before the event takes place. He always tries to be the master of events and not a slave to them.

The ideological foundations for "positive action" are present even in his *Towards Colonial Freedom* written in 1947. He debunks as "incoherent nonsense" the views that imperialism prepares peoples for self-government or has a moral conscience to which the colonial peoples can appeal. He then asserts that "the only thing left for the colonial peoples to do is to *obtain* their freedom and independence from these colonial powers" (p. xviii). Again at pp. 28–29, he writes: "We therefore repeat that *only* the united movement of colonial peoples, determined to assert its right to independence, can compel any colonial power to lay down its 'white man's burden.' . . ." And the *Declaration to the Colonial Peoples of the World,* written by Nkrumah and adopted by the Pan-African Congress in 1945, has this to say: "The object of imperialist powers is to exploit. By granting the right to colonial peoples to govern themselves, they are defeating that objective. Therefore, the struggle for political power by colonial and subject peoples is the first step. . . ." And it adds significantly: "We say to the peoples of the colonies that they must strive for these ends *by all means* at their disposal."

CHAPTER TWO

Consolidation of People's Power

The general law of imperialism is to resist the advance of the national liberation movement described in the first chapter. Every effort is made to undermine and break up the struggle of the colonial peoples for political freedom. The methods used include inducement, detention, imprisonment of the leaders, the banning of organizations, the proscription of literature, the denial of basic human rights of freedom of speech, of assembly and of demonstration.

The methods also include moves to divide the national liberation movement. And this resort to the division of the colonial struggle becomes the major weapon of imperialism the stronger the demand for independence grows. Nkrumah puts it clearly in his book *Africa Must Unite* (the source book for this chapter): "As the nationalist struggle deepens in the colonial territories and independence appears on the horizon, the imperialist powers, fishing in the muddy waters of communalism, tribalism and sectional interests, endeavor to create fissions in the national front, in order to achieve fragmentation" (p. 173).

The state of affairs *inside* the national liberation movement creates the objective conditions for the operation of this imperialist strategy. Making up the national liberation movement are usually two groups of people—"the moderates of the professional and 'aristocratic' class and the so-called extremists of the mass movement" (p. 180).

The "moderates" want "some share in their government" but they are afraid to shoulder the full responsibility of self-government. Accordingly, they are "prepared to leave the main areas of sovereignty to the colonial power in return for a promise of economic aid."

The "extremists" want no partnership with the colonial power and demand full responsibility for the fate of their country "in the belief that even good government is no substitute for self-government."

Naturally, imperialism backs the "moderates" against the "extremists" in the colonial struggle. And the outcome of this struggle is of the greatest importance to the national liberation movement.

If the "moderates" and their imperialist allies win, the end product is a regime of neo-colonialism. On the other hand, victory for the "extremists" opens the way to full independence.

How does imperialism manipulate the national liberation movement in order to produce a regime of neo-colonialism? "Its mechanics are simple. In the dynamics of national revolution there are usually two local elements: the moderates of the professional and 'aristocratic' class and the so-called extremists of the mass movement. . . . Having learnt from experience that the greater and more bitter their resistance to 'extremist' demands for independence the more extreme and more powerful they become, certain colonial powers began to respond more positively to signs of nationalist stirrings in some of their territories. The understanding dawned that in the absence of a bitter struggle, there is a chance of treating with the moderate leaders. . . . The colonial power, experienced in the ways of diplomacy, seeks to curb the efforts of the extremists by ostentatiously polishing the silver platter on which they promise to hand over independence. Underneath the shining surface is the dross. Only the outward form is changed, the intrinsic relationship is maintained" (pp. 179–80).

If the maneuver succeeds, neo-colonialism takes the place of colonialism.

The teachings of Kwame Nkrumah show that such a regime, outwardly independent but inwardly based on the old colonial economic relationships, cannot be described as being independent. He refers to such states as "semi-independent states" (p. 180); as "apparently independent states who serve the interests of the new imperialism, which seeks to salvage something from the wreck of the old imperialism" (p. 181); as "patron-client relationship" (p. 176).

In these states of neo-colonialism, the struggle for freedom is still very much alive. It has to be. For the main contradictions of imperialism still exist. The problem here is not the consolidation of independence but of winning independence.

Neo-colonialism, Nkrumah writes, "is a phenomenon against which all African freedom fighters must be on their guard and resist to the utmost" (p. 181). And the *recipe* put out in the last chapter about organizing and leading a national liberation movement applies to such states.

In addition, a weapon against neo-colonialism is political union of Africa which will enable these states to overcome their economic, financial and military dependence on the imperialist powers.

It is useful to ask the question: Why do the "moderates" win in some countries while the "extremists" win in others? No doubt many factors are involved, including the soundness and effectiveness of those directing imperialist strategy in the country concerned.

But the most important factor is to be found inside the national liberation movement itself. Its structure and composition, its leadership, its motive forces, its ideological content are decisive.

The more it draws on the workers, peasants and youth for its leadership and motive force the greater the chances of winning through to real independence. Conversely, to entrust the leadership of the national liberation movement wholly or principally to a "professional and aristocratic class" and to keep the masses out of active participation in the struggle is to prepare the way for the betrayal of the national liberation movement and to sow the seeds of neo-colonialism.

As soon as the "extremists" lead the national liberation movement to victory, the next stage is the consolidation of the political power of the people. The rest of this chapter is devoted to Nkrumah's teachings on the problems connected with the consolidation of the people's power.

The starting point in this process of consolidation is the constitutional legacy handed over by imperialism as a condition for the grant of independence. "It is becoming axiomatic that colonial powers do not willingly retire from political control over any given land. Before they go they make superhuman efforts to create schisms and rivalries which they hope to exploit after they have gone" (p. 57). These "schisms" are usually built into the constitution and their purpose is to help out "the strategy of divide and rule wielded from afar" (p. 57).

The exact nature of these schisms

embedded in the constitution for independence will vary from one country to another. But, broadly, they aim at three separate objectives which taken together mean the preservation of imperialist interests in the newly emergent state.

These objectives are *constitutional rigidity* which will hamper speedy development, *political separatism* which will hinder the process of evolving an organic and united nation, and a *civil service* apparatus insulated from the new political power in the young state and holding it to ransom at will.

In the period of consolidation, every change is directed towards securing the interests of the masses; and the support of the people must be obtained for every new advance.

This well-nigh deification of the masses is an important element in Nkrumah's teachings. It guarantees every advance because the people, who welcome it, are prepared to defend it against saboteurs and counter-revolutionaries. Again, it creates a favorable impression outside the country concerned thus satisfying an important condition for securing much-needed assistance for rapid economic development.

The process of consolidation must aim at attaining the following objectives:

supremacy of the people;
national unity and stability;
traditional institutions should be made to serve the people;
the civil service must become a vehicle of the revolution;
the pattern of foreign aid must help the onward march.

The first four objectives are met by a new people's constitution supplemented with a few laws. The fifth is attained through sound economic and foreign policies by the government.

The supremacy of the people is achieved through what Nkrumah terms a "people's Parliamentary Democracy." The system is based on a constitution approved by the entire people in a national referendum. The constitution creates a parliament which is "sovereign and unlimited in its enactment of laws" (p. 66) and gives the franchise for electing members of parliament to every man and woman of voting age.

"The laws enacted by parliament are binding upon the people and the government" (p. 66). By this arrangement parliament is supreme; but parliament itself is the creation of the entire people who enjoy free franchise without any discrimination of any sort.

National unity and stability are needed in order to eliminate the conditions favorable to continued imperialist machination and influence. "In fledgeling states, imperialist interests flourish where there is an atmosphere of dissension. They are endangered in an atmosphere of national unity and stability" (p. 76).

The crux of Nkrumah's teachings on achieving national unity and stability is the creation of *national* political institutions. Under this formula, sectional politics (based on religion or tribe) are proscribed. The Ghana Avoidance of Discrimination Law is a case in point. And to compel all aspirants to political power to think in terms of the nation and not of tribe or region, the supremacy of the center (parliament and national government) over the regions is upheld at every turn. It is this that has led Nkrumah to the view that a unitary form of constitution is needed when a young nation is struggling to establish itself and to cover in a few decades the backwardness created by centuries of colonial rule.

It must be pointed out, however, that Nkrumah does not oppose absolutely all forms of regional devolution of powers. He can see the need for some regional authorities. But he insists that regional authority must act in accordance with directives emanating from the center. "A new country needs to initiate central nationwide planning fitting the required activities of each Region into an over-all programme" (p. 64).

This centralized power structure cuts the ground from under the feet of "vested interests" which usually "come to the aid of minority separatist groups" (p. 75). It permits the most efficient use to be made of the scant resources of trained manpower—a handicap which every state emerging from colonial rule invariably suffers.

A new constitution is essential in order "to create an environment in which to proceed more positively with national reconstruction" (p. 85). It is also necessary as an outward expression of a nation's coming of age, for "people who are independent, free and sovereign make their own constitution" (p. 59).

The new constitution is based on five main principles:

- the elimination of "entrenched clauses" which hinder the young nation's free development;
- an executive head of state;
- effective executive control over the civil service;
- the blending of traditional institutions with the service of the people; and

laying the foundation for a smooth advance to a continental government for all-Africa.

The obnoxious "entrenched clauses" must go because their retention means acquiescing in a constitutional arrangement that favors the continued existence of imperialist interests and influences. A republican constitution is desirable because a monarchy is "out of keeping with the full meaning of independence" (p. 80) and "it symbolized an hierarchical pinnacle that no longer had reality in the Ghana-Britain relationship."

An executive president is ideal because it permits the exercise of the "positive leadership that is so vital to a country seeking to pull itself up by its bootstraps" (p. 82). It accords with the African's understanding. For Africans "associate primacy with power" (p. 82) and a "titular president" has no real meaning to a student of democracy.

Perhaps the strongest argument against a "titular president" is that young nations, in the process of nation building, have need for a rallying personality who personifies the aspirations of the people. This, of course, must be carefully distinguished from dictatorship. The dictator sets himself up *against* the people; while the "rallying personality" needed by emerging nations must be the free choice of the people.

Effective executive control over the civil service is achieved through vesting the president with powers of posting, appointment and dismissal, particularly at the policy-making levels. This is an important lever in converting the old colonial civil service built to suit the needs of colonialism into an effective instrument of dynamic change and national reconstruction.

The steady transformation of the human content of the civil service is achieved through a post-graduate institute of public administration which trains new entrants to higher posts in the service.

Traditional institutions, especially

chieftaincy, were used in the colonial era to buttress colonial rule. They formed part of the colonial administrative machinery. Under independence, these institutions must acquire a new orientation. Their existence must be in accord with the will of the people who are supreme.

Nkrumah's prescription is clear-cut: chieftaincy can continue as a transient phenomenon if it "can be used to encourage popular effort." However, he draws attention to "the natural attenuation of chieftaincy under the impact of social progress" (p. 84).

The constitution of people's power must make provision for the surrender of some of the nation's sovereignty "to the total sovereignty of Africa if this should ever be required" (p. 85). This opens the way to an African political union which, in turn, is a condition for the total liberation of Africa and her existence as a powerful and progressive continent free of dependence upon outside forces.

Foreign aid, particularly when it

comes from the imperialist powers, is an important element to be watched in the process of consolidation of the people's power. The sort of aid received could even restrict the unfettered advance of the new state towards economic independence, which is an important objective of the national liberation movement.

It is becoming well known that foreign aid can be administered in such a way as to give foreign investors great control and even direction over a nation's economy. Nkrumah warns against this and asserts: "The pattern of imperialist aid to Africa is set not only to draw the unwary *back into neo-colonialist relationship* but to tie them into cold-war politics" (p. 183).

Finally, the one-party system. Nkrumah sees the emergence of the one-party system as quite natural under certain circumstances. The first condition is that independence should bring into power the "extremist" wing of the national liberation movement (the people's party) which demands political freedom as the key to social reconstruction and the creation of a socialist society.

If the "moderates" of the intellectual and aristocratic class get into power, a neo-colonialist regime comes into being and a second party must come into being to push the national liberation movement to complete victory.

The second condition is that the government of the people's party should achieve "improvements in economic and social conditions" (p. 70) of the masses.

The third condition is that the constitution should give effective power to the people in their generality.

If these conditions are fulfilled, the popularity of the party that brings freedom (in the sense of political freedom and social reconstruction leading to socialism) is enhanced and its majority in parliament grows.

The opposition on the other hand continues to dwindle and soon ceases to be a political force of any consequence. A resort to terrorism is in effect a death gasp, for such tactics can only achieve positive and lasting results where the people generally support the party using it.

It must be pointed out that, if the three conditions given by Nkrumah are fulfilled, there can be no room for a two-party system under existing African conditions. For the second party must demand a return to capitalism which the people have already rejected.

In the alternative, the second party will confine its claims to its ability to perform more efficiently tasks being carried out by the first party. But this is a function which could quite easily be performed *inside* the first party. Thus the two-party system, *given Nkrumah's conditions,* becomes either a retrograde nuisance or an expensive luxury. In either case it meets no social need.

CHAPTER THREE

Socialist Development

There is a school of thought in newly emergent nations which holds the view that the liberation struggle comes to an end when political freedom is won. The protagonists of this view feel that "having made the supreme and sustained effort called for in ridding the country of colonial rule, a well-earned rest can now be taken." Nkrumah regards this view as not only wrong but also as extremely dangerous.

For to leave untouched or to fail to achieve a radical structural recast of the national economy is to create conditions very favorable for the existence of neo-colonialism.

On the contrary, Nkrumah teaches that ahead of a people who have recently emerged from direct colonial rule is "a more formidable battle" in which "a new and greater effort is demanded to consolidate the nationalist victory." This, of course, is a re-statement of the third objective of the national liberation movement defined as *"Social Reconstruction,* i.e. freedom from poverty and economic exploitation and the improvement of social and economic conditions of the people so that they will be able to find better means of achieving and asserting their right to human life and happiness" (*Towards Colonial Freedom,* p. 43).

But freedom from poverty, improvement of social and economic conditions, etc. depend on the coming into existence of a new industrial economy in place of the old colonial economy; for "poverty is progressively reduced only as productivity increases and industrialization progresses and part of its surplus can be made available in increased wages, better housing and generally improved social conditions" (*Africa Must Unite,* p. 106).

Nkrumah holds that the drive towards economic reconstruction must proceed along "the socialist path." He asserts emphatically that "socialism is our only alternative" (p. 119). And this fact is of fundamental importance in Nkrumah's teachings and constitutes a veritable watershed between his ideas on nation-building and those of many contemporary African leaders.

Nkrumah gives three reasons for this view. Firstly, for a developing nation to follow the capitalist path of development means that control of the national economy remains in the hands of foreign private capital. The inevitable result is a neo-colonialist regime because "colonial rule precluded that accumulation of capital among our citizens which would have assisted thorough-going private investment in industrial construction" (p. 119).

Secondly, the colonial regime had to set up some publicly-owned enterprises "capitalized out of national funds." Examples of this are the railways, harbors and electric power. These services should continue to be publicly owned and run, for to hand them over to private interests is to betray "the trust of the great masses of our people to the greedy interests of a small coterie of individuals, probably in alliance with foreign capitalists" (p. 119).

The third reason is that "production for private profit deprives a large section of the people of the goods and services produced" (p. 119).

Post-independence economic reconstruction covers a long and difficult period. It could last a few generations. It certainly stretches over a few decades, judged by experience elsewhere. But, broadly, this period could be divided into three interlocked stages. The first is the period of reconstruction pure and simple when the government concentrates on expanding communications and improving educational and health conditions—the infrastructure for economic growth. During the second stage the main effort is directed towards achieving economic independence; and this in turn lays the foundation for the advance, in the third stage, towards a socialist society.

It is important to see these various stages as forming the organic parts of an evolving process. And because achievements or failures in one stage greatly condition development in a subsequent stage, it is of the greatest importance that the socialist objective of economic reconstruction be fully accepted at the very early stages. A "non-ideological" approach to economic development leads to confusion and the strengthening of externally directed capitalism.

A school of thought advocates that the state in a newly emergent nation should confine its contributions to economic reconstruction, and general development to the provision of the infrastructure for economic activity and social services for the people. It terms such an arrangement the welfare state.

Nkrumah debunks this line of thought by pointing out that: "The welfare state is the climax of a highly developed industrialism. To assure its benefits in a less developed country is to promise merely the division of poverty" (p. 105).

For it is unrealistic to leave the national economy to foreign private capital and at the same time to expect it to provide a tax revenue big enough to support comprehensive social services for the entire people.

Having established that the socialist road to reconstruction and economic development is the best for newly emergent nations, Nkrumah proceeds to expound the principles that underline such a process. His ideas, in this regard, are to be found in his book *Africa Must Unite,* to which all further references in this chapter are made. The rest of this chapter deals with his principles of socialist development.

First, the state must play the major role in economic activity. "Because colonialism prevented the emergence of a strong local capitalist class, because production for private profit is based on exploitation, and because the less developed nations need a high rate of economic growth, the government is obliged to play the role of main entrepreneur in laying the basis of national economic and social advancement" (p. 119).

Other factors that must influence the approach to economic development are the need to break "the European monopoly domination of our economy," the necessity for being "extremely vigilant in scenting out the subtle and insidious infiltrations of neo-colonialism," the ever-present "danger of sabotage by foreigners enjoying . . . the privilege of building economic enterprises in our midst" (p. 102), and the compelling need for stimulating within the country "capital accumulation for re-employment in wider development."

All these considerations reinforce Nkrumah's conclusion that "the government has to take the place of the adventurous entrepreneurs who created the capital basis of industrialization in the advanced countries" (p. 110).

Secondly, national economic planning is the principal lever for all-round progress. In view of the fact that practically all nations today talk of planning, Nkrumah has carefully depicted the features that make up his notion of planning. Planning must cover the entire country and "stretch out into the regions beyond the main centres."

It must be all-embracing, that is comprising economic and general development with plans for "our educational, social welfare and health programmes." It must reflect "the strictest control to safeguard against unrelated overspending on any project" but "there must be a certain elasticity to allow for emendation or adjustment without upsetting the general plan and our budgeting."

Planning must seek to control the re-investment in the country concerned of profits made by firms (foreign and local) operating there. This revolutionary aspect Nkrumah defends thus: "Government interference in all matters affecting economic growth in less developed countries is today a universally accepted principle, and interests, domestic or foreign, enjoying the opportunities of profitable gain, cannot object to *some control of the re-investment of part of that gain* in the national development of the country in which it is reaped" (p. 120).

Another important feature of planning as conceived by Nkrumah is that the part played by the State in economic activities should be an increasing one. "Our planning will be geared to our policy of *increasing governmental participation* in the nation's economic activities, and all enterprises are expected to accept this policy. . . ." (p. 120).

Thirdly, national planning must be geared to socialism. There is a great amount of confused thought on what constitutes socialist planning. In some cases "planning" has been used as an instrument for establishing or boosting capitalism. In the light of this, Nkrumah's teachings clearly elucidate those elements which when taken together constitute socialist planning. These are enumerated as follows:

(1) *A mixed economy.* The economic system is divided into several sections with the state controlling the activities of all sectors through the national plan which it prepares. In Ghana, there are five sectors—state enterprises, enterprises owned by foreign private interests, enterprises jointly owned by state and foreign private interests, cooperatives, enterprises exclusively reserved for Ghanaian private entrepreneurs. A vital consideration here is that each sector operates within limits set by the state. If this is absent, a mixed economy may lead, not to socialism, but to capitalism. Again the state sectors must continually expand. "The socialist base of the economy extends through increasing public ownership of the means of production" (p. 123).

(2) *New institutions (or agencies) for economic activity must be created to replace colonial institutions.* To rely on the old colonial agencies of economic

activity is merely to maintain and even increase the dominant role of colonial relationships in our economic system. It leads to a system of neo-colonialism.

(3) *Relations in agriculture must be recast in order to allow a big upsurge in agricultural production and productivity.* This is "a major priority." Agriculture should be diversified and modernized. Its objectives must be to meet the "needs of the domestic market" and "to provide raw materials for secondary industries." In this way, skills are developed and foreign exchange is saved for financing our industrialization program. The methods used to create the new agriculture which is "a pre-condition for our industrial growth" include grants for capital works (water projects, soil conservation and improvement projects), experimental plantations of new crops, experimental stations for application of new techniques to old crops, free expert advice to farmers on land use, increased productivity and higher yields, hire purchase of farm equipment used as

a lever to encourage cooperative farming, and more efficient marketing.

(4) *The nation itself should be the main source of development capital.* "Surpluses must be pressed out of rising production to finance development" (p. 123). This means that the population must "forgo some immediate personal desire for a greater benefit a bit later on."

(5) *Guarantee of a basic minimum standard of living for all.* This basic minimum Nkrumah describes as, "prices of goods should not exceed wages; house rentals must be within the means of all groups; social welfare services must be open to all; educational and cultural amenities must be available to everyone" (p. 119). Advantages accruing to workers should preferably take the form of increased amenities rather than of higher wages which could lead to inflation and price spirals.

(6) *A steady build-up of trained manpower.* Even where certain services would be more cheaply provided by foreign companies, they are still useful

because they help in rearing skills locally. "An essential element in our industrial development must be the building up of our store of technical and managerial knowledge" (p. 111).

(7) *Industrial planning* should encourage the setting up of those plants in which "we have a natural advantage in local resources and labor or where we can produce essential commodities required for development or for domestic consumption" (p. 111).

(8) *Investment policy should promote the growth of local industries.* To this end investment priority should be determined by the rate of capital formation, savings on imports, boost on exports, and reduction of development gaps between various parts of the country created by colonial exploitation.

(9) *Active participation of the people through their own organizations in the process of economic planning and development.* This is essential for effective democracy, since "control of the modern state is linked up with the con-

trol of the means of production and distribution" (p. 129). Here Nkrumah attaches great importance to trade union and party groups "in factories, workshops, government departments and offices" which must constantly study "party ideology, decisions and programmes" and also explain "government policies and actions" (p. 131). The other important contribution of the people is voluntary service which could help literacy campaigns, and programs for "building of schools, roads, drains, clinics, post offices, houses and community centres." This too requires "the wholehearted support and self-identification of the people" (p. 103).

The fourth principle of socialist development is that foreign capital must be obtained in a manner that will leave full economic control in the hands of the emergent nation. Nkrumah asserts that a foreign company operating for profit in an under-developed country "has nothing to do with aid" (p. 102).

However, our circumstances demand

that we seek capital from outside. The crux of the problem therefore is not that capital comes in from abroad, but rather *the terms* on which such capital comes in. The ideal arrangement is for foreign capital to go into partnership with state enterprises and train local personnel for executive and technical posts at all levels.

We must always seek terms that will "preserve integrity and sovereignty without crippling economic or political ties to any country, bloc or system" (p. 102). And as a general formula Nkrumah states: "Foreign capital is thus useful and helpful if it takes the form of a loan or credit to enable the borrowing country to buy what it needs from whatever sources it likes, and at the same time to retain control of the assets to be developed" (p. 101).

Fifthly, the diversification of foreign economic links. This enables a country to avoid the dangers of "crippling ties to any one country" and helps in the drive for stable and better prices for our primary commodities on the world's markets. It must be pointed out that "stable and high" world prices for our products will increase the surpluses that could be ploughed into industrialization. It will also put economic planning on a firmer footing.

Sixthly, some of the more deleterious social attitudes of the people must be changed. Nkrumah draws attention to the drag on economic activity of the extended family system and the habit of squandering large sums of money on social festivities.

He demands a new spirit of hard work, and savings for production not for festivals.

He adds: "Our less energetic society must be goaded into the acceptance of the stimuli necessary to rapid economic development by alterations in our social relationships and habits, if necessary by law" (p. 105).

Seventh, the rise of a new privileged class must be prevented. Nkrumah here draws attention to the danger of a bourgeois class arising after independence. This class grows up through the contact of its members with the state apparatus. And thus comes into being what some writers term "bureaucratic capitalism" or an "administrative bourgeoisie."

Nkrumah's famous "Dawn Broadcast" of April 8, 1961, is the classic attack on this privileged class which, he maintains, must not be allowed to grow up. "We are setting our hands as firmly as we can against the growth of a privileged section" (p. 103). And again, "I spoke of the dangers arising from Ghanaian public men attempting to combine business with political life, and warned that those who could not give entirely disinterested service should leave politics or be thrown out. Legislation has since limited the amount of property our public men may own" (p. 125).

Eighth, a new budgetary and fiscal system totally different from what obtained in the colonial era must be evolved. The criteria of this new system must be a release of initiative for economic production, the husbanding of national financial resources, the efficient and effective direction of investment for national development, and the prevention of the flight of capital away from the country.

In the performance of these tasks, the new fiscal system will use the state budget, import control, the state bank and an investment bank as its principal weapons.

Ninth, the party of the people must play a decisive role in the economic drive. "Economic independence and the objective of socialism cannot be achieved without decisive party leadership" (p. 128). But the party must enjoy the support of the people and be "imbued with Marxist socialist philosophy." The party plays its part in three distinct ways. It animates its integral wings (trade unions, organizations of farmers, etc.) with the requisites of the drive for economic emancipation. It creates "study groups" in every factory, office, department or workshop to help in the implementation of the state plan, in reporting progress and in supplying valuable views for drawing up the state plan itself.

It trains cadres for all aspects of economic and social work, acting on the Nkrumah maxim that "socialism needs socialists to build it." For this purpose a party school is set up (Kwame Nkrumah Institute at Winneba) and "all, from members of the Central Committee, Ministers and high party officials to the lowest propagandist in the field, pass a course at the Institute" (p. 130).

Tenth, a constantly changing administrative machinery. It is necessary "from time to time to make a review of the administrative apparatus" (p. 129), remembering that we got it from a colonial regime committed to a very different purpose from what we seek. We must also realize that we are out to establish a new life in a new society based on modern modes of production. Thus we live "in a period of flux."

We must therefore always be prepared for change, but these changes must secure our objective and never destroy accepted principles. "We must accommodate our minds and attitudes, to the need for constant adaptation, never losing sight of principle and our expressed social objective" (p. 129).

CHAPTER FOUR

African Unity

To Kwame Nkrumah, African unity is a consuming passion. It is at the same time a potent and rational formula for solving the intricate and urgent problems facing Africa and the world. African unity sets the horizon and provides the moving spirit in the teachings of Nkrumah. In it, his entire philosophy lives, and moves and has its being.

It is significant that while in Britain (1945-47) Nkrumah, though in close touch with many African students' organizations, did most of his work with the Pan-African Congress. The resolution written by him and adopted by the Fifth Pan-African Congress in Manchester England, October 1945, was captioned *Declaration to the Colonial Peoples of the World*. And while other African nationalists after World War II concentrated on political programs for their respective countries, Nkrumah's book *Towards Colonial Freedom*, written in 1947, studies the problem of winning freedom for all African colonies. Its battle cry is "Colonial and Subject Peoples of the World—Unite."

The concrete facts of African political life at the time Nkrumah completed his studies overseas and was ready to return to Africa, compelled him to go back to the then Gold Coast, his native country. And for ten years Nkrumah grappled with the problem of leading the national liberation movement in one country. But, as events have since proved, Nkrumah far from abandoning his Africa perspective, was merely creating a base on African soil for the more energetic pursuit of his plan for all Africa. Testimony of this was given on March 6, 1957, when addressing a vast crowd in Accra on the occasion of the attainment of independence he said: "The independence of Ghana is meaningless until it is linked with the total liberation of Africa."

Barely a year after Ghana's independence, in April 1958, the first conference of Independent African States was held in Accra, on the initiative of Nkrumah. The conference endorsed the concept of African Unity. Specifically, it accepted the following principles:

(1) a common foreign policy based on non-alignment and positive neutrality, pursued through co-ordinated action at the United Nations, and directed towards African freedom and world peace;

(2) coordinated economic development geared to "the establishment of equitable social and economic policies which will provide national prosperity and social security for all citizens";

(3) joint action by independent African states for the liberation of all African territories still under colonial rule;

(4) joint action by independent African States against social discrimination and apartheid.

And by December 1958, again at Accra and on the initiative of Nkrumah, the All-African Peoples Conference, linking political parties and movements in all African countries, was convened. It set up a machinery for giving effective aid, from independent African states to national liberation movements throughout Africa. It characterized neo-colonialism as an even more insidious form of imperialism.

In this way, African unity, after ten years in search of a base on African soil, reemerged as a dynamic concept. It has ever since been the bugbear of imperialism in Africa. In a very real sense, it can be said that African politics since 1958 has been the demands of African unity and the reactions of imperialists and their African allies to these demands.

To Nkrumah, African unity is not

just an end in itself. It is the means to an end "in which freedom and unity can flourish amidst plenty." It is "an inescapable desideratum . . . for creating a modern society which will give our people the opportunity to enjoy a full and satisfying life" (*Africa Must Unite*, p. 221).

Here, Nkrumah differs fundamentally from other great men of history who have advocated unity in their respective areas. Men like Napoleon of France, Garibaldi of Italy and Gamel Ataturk of Turkey sought unity because of the state power and military grandeur it conferred. Nkrumah, on the other hand, seeks African unity for the benefits it would confer on the African peoples and on mankind as a whole. This socialist orientation is the bedrock of his teachings on African unity.

Nkrumah sees African unity as the most effective weapon for attaining three principal objectives:

(1) total liberation of Africa from colonial rule;

(2) fighting neo-colonialism in the independent African states;

(3) creating world conditions favorable to African prosperity and independence and the happiness of mankind.

We shall examine these three objectives in turn. Nkrumah teaches that unity among independent African states is the most powerful lever for hastening the end of colonial rule everywhere in Africa. He bases this view on two principles, both embodied in the "Resolution on the Future of Dependent Territories in Africa," adopted at the 1958 Accra Conference of Independent African States.

The first principle is that "the existence of colonialism in any shape or form is a threat to the security and independence of the African states and to world peace."

The second principle flows logically from the first. It is that "the problems and the future of dependent territories in Africa are not the exclusive concern of the colonial powers but the responsibility of all members of the United Nations and in particular of the Independent African States."

The tactics advocated by Nkrumah in the pursuit of the objective of freeing Africa from colonial rule consist of diplomatic action at the UN, "all possible assistance" to the national liberation movements, and the offer of facilities for training and educating people of the colonial territories. While the first tactic is pursued by independent African states at the UN, acting in concert, the other two tactics are carried out through the All-African Peoples' Conference which links independent African states with the national liberation movements in the colonial territories.

Secondly, fighting neo-colonialism. Neo-colonialism manifests itself in military pacts, military bases on African soil, unfair economic agreements, domination of African public services by non-African personnel and one-sided trade arrangements. Nkrumah's view is that the unity of independent African states will create an African state big enough and powerful enough to eliminate all these handicaps. It will also remove frontier disputes which provide a convenient cover for imperialist maneuvers directed against the sovereignty and security of independent African states. It will either provide Africa with the necessary capital resources out of its own domestic sources or will enable foreign capital to be attracted on terms more advantageous to Africa than at present. Hence, African unity aims at complete independence for the sovereign African states.

Thirdly, the creation of world conditions favorable to Africa's independence and security, and to the progress of mankind. This is achieved by a united Africa teaming up with other nations to expand the area of non-alignment in the world. For, "the more unaligned nations there are, the wider the non-committed area of the world, the better the chances of human survival" (*Africa Must Unite*, pp. 199–200).

World peace, Nkrumah teaches, is the condition for rapid and independent development in Africa and also for human survival and progress. And the most effective way to achieve world peace, considering the existence of two powerful armed blocs, is to create a zone of uncommitted nations and steadily to expand this zone. Neutrality, therefore, is positive not negative. It is active not passive. It reaches out to create conditions favorable for our needs. It is not isolationist and introspective. Writing about war, which can destroy both the participants and non-participants alike, Nkrumah asserts that "negative neutralism is no shield at all. It is completely impotent and even dangerous" (*Africa Must Unite,* p. 200).

Nkrumah's approach to world peace is not pacifist. He maintains that the only road to lasting peace is the elimination of the causes of war. He brings out this view clearly in *Africa Must Unite,* where he asserts that "world peace is not possible without the complete liquidation of colonialism and the total liberation of peoples everywhere"

(p. 203). And while advocating "peaceful coexistence" because of the "balance of forces in the world today," Nkrumah maintains that "until colonialism and imperialism in all their various forms and manifestations have been completely eradicated from Africa, it would be inconsistent for the African Revolution to coexist with imperialism" (p. 204).

What is the content of Nkrumah's concept of African unity? We know the objectives of African unity both on the African continent and in the world at large. But what principles make up his concept of African unity?

These are three: overall economic planning, unified military and defense strategy, and unified foreign policy and diplomacy.

Overall economic planning on a continental basis would increase the industrial and economic power of Africa. The resources of Africa would be used to the best advantage. And an all-African central bank of issue will be a most effective instrument "to re-orientate the economy of Africa and place it beyond the reach of foreign control" (p. 219). Thus overall economic planning will give Africa the much needed economic independence in a very short time.

This view of economic development rejects the traditional concept of dependence on foreign powers, especially on the former colonial powers. It makes Africans responsible for Africa's economy and completely rejects the notion of Africa being an economic appendage of Europe or America. In Nkrumah's own words: "We in Africa have looked *outwards* too long for the development of our economy. Let us begin to look *inwards* into the African continent for all aspects of its development" (p. 219).

A unified military and defense strategy is demanded in Africa today because no single African state can protect its sovereignty against an imperialist aggressor, because apartheid is arming for a future attempt to crush African nationalism by force, because military expenditure is too heavy a burden for Africa's young nations faced with pressing problems of development.

The only alternative to unified defense and strategy is the conclusion of military pacts with foreign powers. And these military pacts provide the conditions for continued interference of non-African powers in African life and development. Nkrumah warns: "If we do not unite and combine our military resources for common defence, the individual states, out of a sense of insecurity, may be drawn into making defence pacts with foreign powers which *may endanger the security of us all"* (p. 220).

And a unified foreign policy and diplomacy follows logically on the first two types of joint action because it is necessary "to give political direction to our joint efforts for the protection and economic development of our continent" (p. 220). Here it must be emphasized that all talk of effective and large-scale joint action between African states is wishful thinking if there is no agreement on political issues. The reasoning here is self-evident. For all actions in the fields of the economy and defense are guided by political decisions.

This raises a vital issue in the big debate on African unity. Which should come first, political unity or cooperation in limited spheres? It is obvious that cooperation in limited spheres must be based on political decisions. Otherwise, it cannot go beyond the level of normal intercourse between sovereign states. The wisdom of Nkrumah's line of going straight for political unity is becoming increasingly clear and compelling.

But, apart from imperialist intrigues to resist African political union which is a threat to the whole position of imperialism on the African continent, some African states are reluctant to part with their newly-won sovereignty.

Nevertheless, Nkrumah has an answer even to this problem. He calls for an African Parliament (Upper House with equal representation of all states, and a Lower House with representation according to population) with clearly defined powers. All other powers are reserved to the member states in the exercise of which each state is sovereign. Economic planning, defense and foreign affairs he allocates to the African Government leaving all other powers to individual African states which will continue to have their national flag, national anthem, national coat of arms and all other appurtenances of an independent sovereign state.

Nkrumah's formula is explained by him in the following words: "I am confident that it should be possible to devise a constitutional structure applicable to our special conditions in Africa . . . which will enable us to secure the objectives I have defined [over-all economic planning, unified military and defense strategy, unified foreign policy and diplomacy—*ed.*] and yet preserve to some extent the sovereignty of each state within a union of African states" (*Africa Must Unite*, p. 220).

Nkrumah is a socialist. World experience has shown how difficult it is to build socialism in a country surrounded by hostile capitalist states. This task is almost impossible in a small underdeveloped country enveloped in a big land mass firmly held by imperialism either in the form of colonialism or neo-colonialism.

African unity, according to Nkrumah, will create some of the necessary objective conditions for the rapid advance towards socialism not only in a single African state but throughout the African continent. Here the struggle for African unity becomes in reality another form of the battle between socialism and imperialism on the African continent.

CHAPTER FIVE

The Party

It has been shown that Kwame Nkrumah is a revolutionary who lives and works in a revolutionary era. His efforts have been directed towards the overthrow of colonial rule, towards the achieving of economic independence, towards the building of a socialist state in Ghana, and towards African unity.

In all these struggles Nkrumah sees the sustaining and all-conquering force as the masses knit together in revolutionary action. Nkrumah has unbounded faith in the masses; and the central thesis in all his actions as a political leader is the organization of the masses around a clearly defined program and for the full realization of that program.

Nkrumah holds that the revolutionary initiative of the masses can move mountains. And the party is the concrete expression—the organizational form—of this revolutionary initiative. Hence, for Nkrumah, the right type of party is of the greatest importance to the success of the national, the socialist and the African revolutions. "Looking back, and trying to determine the reasons for the successful outcome of our struggle for freedom, one factor stands out above all others, namely, the strength of a well-organized political party, representative of the broad masses of the people . . . in daily, living touch with the ordinary mass of the people it represented. . . ." (*Africa Must Unite*, p. 54).

Again, while discussing the drive towards socialism in Ghana, Nkrumah writes: "Just as political independence could not have been attained without the leadership of a strong, disciplined party, so Ghana's economic independence and the objective of socialism cannot be achieved without decisive party leadership" (*Africa Must Unite*, p. 128).

Elsewhere (*Africa Must Unite*, p. 50) Nkrumah describes the party as "an essential forger of the political revolution," thus showing that there can be no real and lasting revolution without a strong and well-organized political party to guide and lead it.

Having pointed out the great importance attached to the party by Nkrumah, the rest of this chapter is devoted to the exposition of his views on the nature, the style of work, the objectives and the methods of the party.

The common man is the pivot of Nkrumah's concept of the party. Speaking at the Accra Arena on June 12, 1949—the day the Convention People's Party was formally inaugurated—Nkrumah expressed the view that "out of the simple man is ordained strength."

This was a fundamental departure from the views held by political leaders of the time, men who believe in caucus political organizations of intellectuals with their clientele of businessmen and chiefs. The party lives with the common man, discusses his problems, shares his aspirations, and organizes him to fight his own battles for his salvation. In short, in the masses the party lives and moves and has its being.

This view of the party as the vanguard of the masses, the fighting organization of the people, animated by the initiative of the people and directed towards serving the people is older than the CPP.

In the resolution written by Nkrumah and adopted as *Declaration to the Colonial Peoples of the World* by the Fifth Pan-African Congress, we read: "Today there is only one road to effective action—the organization of the masses."

And on January 20, 1948, as general secretary of the United Gold Coast Convention (UGCC), Nkrumah submitted a program of organization to the Working Committee of the Convention. This idea of building upon the masses comes out clearly in the following points contained in Nkrumah's memorandum on reorganization:

Organizational Work:
The organizational work of implementing the platform of the Convention will fall into three periods:

First period:
- (a) Coordination of all the various organizations under the United Gold Coast Convention: i.e., apart from individual membership, the various political, social, educational, farmers' and women's organizations as well as native societies, trade unions, cooperative societies, etc., should be asked to affiliate to the Convention.
- (b) The consolidation of branches already formed and the establishment of branches in every town and village of the country will form another major field of action during the first period.
- (c) Convention branches should be set up in each town and village

throughout the colony, Ashanti, the Northern Territories and Togoland. The chief or Odikro of each town or village should be persuaded to become the Patron of the branch.

(d) Vigorous Convention week-end schools should be opened wherever there is a branch of the Convention. The political mass education of the country for self-government should begin at these week-end schools.

Second Period:

To be marked by constant demonstrations throughout the country to test our organizational strength, making use of political crises.

Third Period:

(a) The convening of a Constitutional Assembly of the Gold Coast people to draw up the Constitution for self-government or national independence.

(b) Organized demonstration, boycott and strike—our only weapons to support our pressure for self-government.

And in *Ghana: The Autobiography of Kwame Nkrumah,* he writes further: "We had succeeded because we had talked with the people and by so doing knew their feelings and grievances" (p. 90).

A study of Nkrumah's writings and actions connected with building the CPP reveals certain basic principles underlying his concept of the party. These five basic principles are reviewed briefly hereunder.

First, the party membership is open to the entire people. In his own words, it must be a "broadly based political party." And writing about the CPP in his autobiography he states. "We excluded no one. For if a national movement is to succeed, every man and woman of goodwill must be allowed to play a part" (p. 90).

Secondly, the party must have a clear-cut program and an ideology. The party is not an organization around a personality. On the contrary, it organizes the masses around a program based on an acceptable ideology. For Africa the programs must be self-government opening the door to complete independence and a socialist society. Those who wish to lead the peoples' struggle for freedom "must declare their aims openly and unmistakably" (*Africa Must Unite*, p. 50). Again at p. 129, Nkrumah asserts that the CPP is "imbued with Marxist Socialist philosophy."

It is useful to understand the relation between program and ideology. While the ideology maps out the general route to be followed by the party, the program sets out the immediate targets and tasks at every stage in the struggle. Thus ideology is immutable but program is constantly changing, one leading logically and inescapably to the next and so on until the ultimate goal of a socialist society is achieved.

It would be wrong to have a program without an ideology. For as conditions change, it becomes necessary to change the program. And an attempt to draw up a program, if there is no ideology to guide the action, may lead to a break-up of the party. This danger is ever present in a party whose membership is open to all, irrespective of social and economic status.

Thirdly, party education. Because of the necessarily heterogeneous composition of the party, embracing all sections of the people, great reliance must be placed on party education as the instrument for welding this amorphous collection of people into an organic and dedicated body of men and women sharing an identical view of human society. To achieve this objective, party education is conducted at all levels because "every avenue of education and information must be used to stir and nourish the political consciousness of the people" (*Africa Must Unite*, p. 130).

The party runs "refreshe. courses in party political teaching." A party institute of Economic and Political Science is established at Winneba and "is responsible for the party's general political education."

Every party member in a position of trust or where he is called upon to give guidance to others around him goes to the Winneba Institute.

"All, from members of the Central Committee, Ministers and high party officials to the lowest propagandists in the field, pass through a course at the Institute.

"Farmers, factory workers, and others from all walks of life meet at Winneba, where they have the opportunity to broaden their political knowledge and ideological understanding" (*Africa Must Unite,* pp. 130–31).

This is not all. This centralized effort is supplemented with educational activity in widely dispersed factories and farms all over Ghana. "Party study groups exist all over the country, in factories, workshops, government departments and offices, in fact, in every nook and cranny of Ghana, for the study of African life and culture, party ideology, decisions and programs, and for explaining government policies and actions" (*Africa Must Unite,* p. 131).

Fourthly, democratic centralism.
This is the organizational principle on which the whole party edifice is built. It means simply that at every level the people freely elect all organs of the party. And flowing from this, all lower organs of the party must follow the directives of the higher organs; and the entire party membership must follow the directives of the Central Committee of the party.

Fifthly, the supremacy of the party.
This is the principle on which party discipline is built. And it ties up with the earlier principle of democratic centralism. For Nkrumah, the party must be obeyed by all its members because the organs issuing the directives are elected by the members themselves.

Obedience to the party is not sought on the fascist concept that it represents divine will revealed only to the leader or fuehrer. The rank and file obey directives because these emanate from party organs elected by the rank and file and the organ itself is bound by a program and an ideology which the rank and file had freely adopted. Discipline is accordingly high because it is not mechanical. Rather it is conscious and self-imposed.

Nkrumah teaches that a closely knit political party organized on the principles discussed above should pursue the conquest of political power with singleness of purpose and with dedication.

He rejects collaboration with the enemy absolutely. "A policy of collaboration and appeasement would get us nowhere in our struggle for immediate self-government" (*Autobiography*, p. 85).

He also rejects the policy of putting development before conquest of political power. "Every movement for independence in a colonial situation contains two elements: the demand for political freedom and the revolt against poverty and exploitation. Resolute leadership is required to subordinate the understandable desire of the people for better living conditions to the achievement of the primary aim of the abolition of colonial rule" (*Africa Must Unite*, p. 51).

This is the famous "seek ye first the political kingdom" formula. But, he maintains, political power cannot be won on a silver platter. In *Towards Colonial Freedom,* Nkrumah states: "The object of imperialist powers is to exploit. By granting the right to the colonial peoples to govern themselves, they are defeating that objective.

"Therefore, the struggle for political power by colonial and subject peoples is the first step towards, and the necessary pre-requisite to complete social, economic and political emancipation" (pp. 44–45).

The struggle for political power must be based on the initiative of the people, on what Nkrumah terms briefly "positive action." For, "in spite of the moralizings of British colonialists who argue that political reform is granted as and when the colony is ready for it, change has, in fact, come mostly as a result of pressure from below" (*Africa Must Unite,* p. 17).

SOME ESSENTIAL FEATURES OF NKRUMAISM

And what is "Positive Action"? "I described Positive Action as the adoption of all legitimate and constitutional means by which we could attack the forces of imperialism in the country. The weapons were legitimate political agitation, newspaper and educational campaigns and, as a last resort, the constitutional application of strikes, boycotts and non-cooperation based on the principle of absolute non-violence. . . ." (*Autobiography,* p. 92).

In view of the fact that both the strategy and the tactics of the party are based on mass action, it is important to consider Nkrumah's teachings on the mass line of the party. Nkrumah's mass line is based on the following notions:

(1) belief in the revolutionary ability of the masses;
(2) organization of the masses around their needs and aspirations;
(3) learning about the masses by living with the masses;

(4) leading the masses into action to fight for their own demands;

(5) indissoluble ties with all the organizations of the masses.

In the *Accra Evening News* of January 14, 1949, Nkrumah put the case for his mass line as follows: "The strength of the organized masses is invincible.... We must organize as never before, for organization decides everything." And in *Africa Must Unite* (p. 55), he gives his "advice to members of any nationalist and progressive party" in the form of a Chinese poem:

> *Go to the people*
> *Live among them*
> *Learn from them*
> *Love them*
> *Serve them*
> *Plan with them*
> *Start with what they know*
> *Build on what they have*

The pursuit of the mass line in party work means evolving close ties with mass organizations (e.g. trades unions, farmers' and youth organizations) where they exist. Where they do not exist, it is the duty of the party to create and then lead them.

And the leadership of mass organizations by the party is achieved by fighting for leading party cadres in the leadership of such organizations and for the adoption of the party line in these organizations. A condition of success is that the party line must be accurate. It must reflect the needs of the masses and it must be understood by them.

Lastly, the political party in relation to the African revolution. Nkrumah teaches that the struggle for African freedom and unity has reached the stage when Africa should "have a common political party with a common aim and programme" (*Africa Must Unite*, p. 52).

He sees such a continental party as people's parties in every African country cooperating with one another through "a central organization" and a "highly-trained headquarters staff." The common aim and objective of these parties must be "the freedom and unity of Africa." After pointing out that the CPP from its very inception had allowed for cooperation with fraternal parties in Africa and elsewhere, Nkrumah asserts: "If this kind of solidarity on the party political level could be achieved, it would surely strengthen African continental freedom and unity" (*Africa Must Unite*, pp. 52–53).

In the long-run, this might well prove the only sure instrument for winning and consolidating the political unity of all Africa.

CHAPTER SIX

The Philosophy of Our Revolution

Africa needs a philosophy which will be both a rational exposition of her past experiences and an intellectual stimulus to her renaissance. Should Africa seek this in the wholesale, indiscriminate importation of foreign ideologies? Or should Africa turn back on world knowledge in a sort of philosophical isolationism? The first alternative is undesirable because a living philosophy which seeks to explain man's experience and provide a rational guide to his actions must reflect and explain the social milieu in which man finds himself. The second alternative is impossible because, in the final analysis, human knowledge belongs to one world pool and, in any case, Africa, for the past centuries, has become so influenced by various strands of civilization and culture that she just cannot cut herself adrift. What then is the solution?

Africa must evolve a philosophy that can provide the intellectual cohesion we so urgently need. Such philosophy must rationalize and harmonize the dominant intellectual strands in Africa's historical experience, reinstate what was noble and elevating in traditional African society and have itself firmly linked with the common pool of world knowledge. The need is for a new philosophical synthesis which is both general and specific. General, because its intellectual roots can be traced to the common pool of world knowledge. Specific, because it grows out of and seeks to explain and guide the African social milieu.

This new synthesis is philosophical consciencism which is the subject matter of a new book by Kwame Nkrumah, just published.

The world knows Kwame Nkrumah

as a politician, a statesman and as a leading architect and protagonist of the concept of the political unity of Africa. With *Conscwncism: Philosophy and Ideology of Decolonisation and Development* Kwame Nkrumah emerges as a philosopher. This philosophical work is destined to make a big impact on the entire world. Although its driving motive is the reinstitution of the best in the traditional African way of life, its intellectual tools are drawn from world philosophy after a most careful examination and evaluation of various schools of thought. In the process a new philosophy has emerged. It overcomes the conflicts in African intellectual life, provides a positive guide to purposeful action in emergent Africa, and at the same time enriches world knowledge.

Philosophical consciencism upholds the ideology of socialism. Its social milieu is Africa but its application is universal to all dependent countries or emerging nations. Its foundation is materialism impregnated with egalitarianism and an ethical view of man. Its approaches are positive and its methods are dialectical. It is both revolutionary and evolutionary in content, revolutionary if juxtaposed with colonialism and capitalism from which it recoils; evolutionary if considered in relation to the traditional African society whose guiding principles of egalitarianism and the concern of all for each it seeks to reassert and enthrone, and regards as fundamental to any society or social order. Society, Nkrumah points out, implies "a certain dynamic unity." Therefore the purpose of philosophy, which, as we see, should reflect and serve its social milieu, must be to provide "a theoretical basis for the cohesion." This is what *philosophical consciencism* sets out to do for the new Africa now emerging from decades of colonialism and centuries of feudalism.

The other idea basic to Nkrumah's thinking is a new conception of African history. He rejects, in its entirety, that view which regards African history "as the story of European adventures." This distorted viewpoint cuts Africa off from centuries of her glorious past. And it makes it look as if Africa was a historical vacuum until the time of Vasco da Gama, Mungo Park and the piratical horde of European adventurers.

Kwame Nkrumah asserts that African history existed for a very long time before the impact first of Near Eastern-Islamic culture and later of Euro-Christian culture. Each of these civilizations brought its own social, economic and political beliefs and organizations. Islamic civilization, through the Jihad or religious war, brought in its wake the slave society which evolved into feudalism. Euro-Christian civilization was the vehicle for Western industrialism which manifested itself in imperialism, in the forms both of colonialism and neo-colonialism. After centuries of struggle with these alien civilizations, traditional Africa is rediscovering itself in the new independent states of Africa.

By this richer and fuller view of history, both the Islamic and Euro-Christian civilizations are treated as "experiences" of African history. "African society must be treated as enjoying its own integrity; its history must be a mirror of that society, and the European contact must find its place in this history only as an African experience, even if a crucial one." Thus African history can be likened to a single small stream in its upper reaches, which in its middle reaches, corresponding to the impact of alien civilizations, breaks into several channels. But further downstream, corresponding to the attainment of political independence, these various channels are reunited into one mighty river.

It is very helpful to point out at this juncture that Dr. Nkrumah also rejects the narrow view which thinks that African society can simply shed the impact of foreign civilization on it and return smugly to the "pure" African society of old. Such an escapism he sees clearly as impossible and unreal. For "our society is not the old society, but a new society enlarged by Islamic and Euro-Christian influences."

The restitution of African society simply cannot be achieved through a hankering after the economic and political forms of traditional Africa. It must be sought by way of a new "harmony" that will allow for the presence of Islamic and Euro-Christian influence "so that this presence is in tune with the original humanist principles underlying African society."

From this viewpoint socialism becomes a rediscovery, in modern terms, of that communalism which is the bedrock of traditional African society. This communalism manifested itself in equalitarianism and the "responsibility of many for one." Accordingly "socialism can be and is the defense of the principles of communalism in a modern setting."

This dialectical conception of African history and African society leads logically to two conclusions. First, the exploiting society with antagonistic classes—and slavery, feudalism and capitalism are mere variations on this central theme of class exploitation—is alien to traditional African society and a complete break from it. The second conclusion is that socialism and traditional African society can be seen as having a common ideological lineage.

May we now briefly examine aspects of the new philosophy? Its starting point is that "in every society there is to be found an ideology" explicit or implicit. This ideology defines "the desirable society." Even if this conception starts as the view of a group in society, it strives constantly to pervade all aspects of the life of its society. It strives to attain social cohesion on the basis of what it considers the "desirable society."

In this drive for social cohesion, many instruments are employed. Some are open and take the form of "prohibitions and permissions made explicit in a statutory way." Others are indirect and subtle, among which are "class structure, history, literature, art, religion." "Philosophy, too, is one of the subtle instruments of ideology and social cohesion. Indeed, it affords a theoretical basis for the cohesion."

Philosophical consciencism regards socialism as the definition of "the desirable society" in Africa. It then sets out to provide the "theoretical basis" for the ideology of socialism in Africa. Accordingly philosophical consciencism is the intellectual instrument of socialism in Africa.

Why is philosophical consciencism necessary? With the return of political independence to the greater part of Africa, "three broad features" have stamped themselves on our life. "African society has one segment which comprises our traditional way of life; it has a second segment which is filled by the presence of the Islamic tradition in Africa; it has a final segment which represents the infiltration of the Christian tradition and culture of Western Europe into Africa, using colonialism and neo-colonialism as its primary vehicles. These different segments are animated by competing ideologies. But since society implies a certain dynamic unity, there needs to emerge an ideology which, genuinely catering for the needs of all, will take the place of the competing ideologies, and so reflect the dynamic unity of society, and be the guide to society's continual progress."

In other words, three layers of culture and civilization constitute present-day African society. At bottom is the traditional African way of life on which has been superimposed both the Islamic Middle East and the Christian West European systems. These elements are not geographically separate and distinct. Rather they permeate each other over the same geographical area. Hence, the way to the elimination of the conflicting and competing ideologies these generate cannot be by geographical separatism. This has to be sought by way of philosophical synthesis.

Such a synthesis will permit dynamic growth to replace the present state of ideological attrition with its consequent dissipation of energy, its stagnation or very slow rate of progress. It will provide an intellectual fortification for African unity which everyday experience has demonstrated to be an indispensable condition for real progress and advancement on this continent.

And such a philosophical synthesis is consciencism.

It is useful at this stage to make the point that philosophical consciencism treats the Islamic Middle East and Christian West European traditions as experiences of traditional African society. These influences are not the original foundations of African society even though their impact is profound. There was a traditional African society which, through history, came to be greatly influenced by the incursions of both the Islamic and the Christian civilizations.

The traditional African society was based on egalitarianism and humanism. In other words, it regarded men as equal; it saw man as an end and not as a means; it enjoined the concern of all for each. This system has for several centuries been overrun by both Islamic Arabic culture and Christian technological civilization. The result is three Africas, traditional Africa as the base on which stand accretions of Islamic and Euro-Christian Africa.

It is important to note that the present African society is not simply the old one writ large. "Our society is not the old society, but a new society enlarged by Islamic and Euro-Christian influences. A new emergent ideology is therefore required, but at the same time an ideology which will not abandon the original humanist principles of Africa. Such a philosophical statement will be born out of the crisis of the African conscience confronted with the three strands of present African society. Such a philosophical statement I proposed to name philosophical consciencism for it will give the theoretical basis for an ideology whose aim shall be to contain the African experience of Islamic and Euro-Christian presence as well as the experience of the traditional African society, and, by gestation, employ them for the harmonious growth and development of that society."

The cardinal principles of philosophical consciencism can now be summarized. Firstly, it asserts the absolute and independent existence of matter which it defines as "a plenum of forces in tension." Secondly, because it is a plenum of forces in tension, matter is capable of spontaneous self-motion. Thirdly, the motion of matter is not merely unilinear. It is both quantitative and qualitative. Hence the motion of matter is dialectical. Fourthly, both mind and body (spirit and matter) exist, but matter is primary. Between these two there is interaction which is achieved by way of "categorial conversion."

Having chosen its tools for intellectual analysis, philosophical consciencism goes on to assert that knowledge is acquired through practice and enriched by constant observation and study of an environment. ". . . Philosophical consciencism builds itself by becoming a reflection of the objectivity, in conceptual terms, of the unfolding of matter."

However, this connection between knowledge and action is not mechanistic. It reflects matter but impregnates this reflection with ethical rules. For as long as materialism supports egalitarianism on the social plane, it touches on ethics. "Egalitarianism is not only political but also ethical: for it implies a certain range of human conduct which is alone acceptable to it."

We are, however, warned that consciencism "cannot freeze its ethical rules with changelessness" even though these rules issue from an objective study of matter. To it, "ethical rules are not permanent but depend on the stage reached in the historical evolution of a society." But whatever that stage may be and whatever forms ethical rules may take the "cardinal principles of egalitarianism are conserved."

Philosophical consciencism has accordingly built its own moral or ethical theory. Once we accept egalitarianism which derives directly from materialism, then it follows that each man must be treated as an end in himself and not just as a tool or a means to an end. "The cardinal ethical principle of philosophical consciencism is to treat each man as an end in himself and not merely as a means. This is fundamental to all socialist or humanist conceptions of man."

Is it then right to argue that philosophical consciencism assumes certain principles abstractly derived? No. At p. 95 it is strongly asserted that "we derive it (i.e. moral view of man) from a materialist viewpoint." It goes on: "This derivation can be made by way of that egalitarianism which is the social reflection of materialism."

Founding itself squarely on philosophical materialism shot through and through with ethical principles that should govern social practice, philosophical consciencism has evolved its own political theory. Looked at from another angle, the political theory of philosophical consciencism is an application, on the political plane, of philosophical materialism permeated with the ethical theory that enjoins treating each man as an end in himself, and with a social theory based on egalitarianism.

Political consciencism is an absolute revolt against colonialism, imperialism and capitalism. It sees capitalism as "domestic colonialism," and launches a devastating attack on the system. It terms capitalism "the gentleman's method of slavery" which in essence, though not in form, is the lineal descendant of the slave society and of feudalism. It maintains that "capitalism is unjust"; that it is "alien" to Africa; that in newly emergent Africa it is "too complicated to be workable." Therefore, it contends, "capitalism would be a betrayal of the personality and conscience of Africa."

Political consciencism upholds socialism. Even though historically it has appeared on the human scene after capitalism, socialism is not a development from capitalism.

"Rather it stands for the negation of that very principle wherein capitalism has its being, lives, and thrives, that principle which unites capitalism with slavery and feudalism," namely exploitation.

Then we are given the historic and life-giving concept that socialism is in line with the traditional African society. "If one seeks the social-political ancestor of socialism, one must go to communalism. Socialism stands to communalism as capitalism stands to slavery."

But socialism is not merely communalism restated. In socialism, the principles underlying communalism are given expression in modern circumstances. Thus, whereas communalism in an untechnical society can be *"laissez faire,"* in a technical society when sophisticated means of production are at hand, if the underlying principles of communalism are not given centralized and correlated expression, class cleavages will arise, which are connected with economic disparities, and thereby with political inequalities. Socialism, therefore, can be and is the defense of the principles of communalism in a modern setting. Socialism is a form of social organization which, guided by the principles underlying communalism, adopts procedures and measures made necessary by demographic and technological developments.

This is perhaps the greatest contribution of consciencism to political philosophy in emergent Africa. For it establishes in a logical and rational manner the link between the essence of socialism and the quintessence of traditional African life. It thereby saves us from the dangerous intellectual vulgarization which is reflected in what is called "African socialism." Those who use the term "African socialism" because they seek socialism with a distinctly African setting are now provided with an unambiguous platform—philosophical consciencism. Those others who sought to use "African socialism" as a cloak for pushing reactionary imperialist concepts in Africa now stand isolated and exposed.

The basis of political action under consciencism is to maximize positive action. In every society, more so in a colonial and semi-dependent society, there is both positive and negative action. While positive action is progressive and forward impelling, negative action is reactionary and backward looking. These forces can be measured through a "statistical analysis . . . of such facts as production, distribution, income, etc."

The balance existing at any time between these two sets of forces defines the character of the society under consideration. It is this basic conflict of opposites which is the main motive force in society.

"There is a fundamental law of the evolution of matter to higher forms. This evolution is dialectical. And it is also the fundamental law of society. It is out of tension that being is born. Becoming is a tension, and being is the child of that tension of opposed forces and tendencies."

When the sum total of positive action exceeds negative action, a colonial territory transforms into an independent, sovereign state. But after political independence it is also necessary to push on to national reconstitution through positive action of the people. Hence the need at all times to maximize positive action.

This requires a "mass party," which must be "armed with an ideology" and the quality of whose members must be constantly raised by education. In a colonial territory, "positive action must be backed by a mass party, complete with its instruments of education." And to do battle effectively with the forces of negative action, positive action must "seek an alignment of all forces of progress."

We are, however, warned that in pursuing its immediate objectives of defeating colonialism, positive action must protect its own future. "When positive action resorts to an alignment of forces, it creates in itself seams at which this alignment might fall apart. It is essential that positive action should in its dialectical evolution anticipate this seminal disintegration and discover a way of containing the future schismatic tendencies, a way of nipping fragmentation in the bud as colonialism begins to reel and totter under the frontal onslaught of positive action. But even with colonialism worsted, positive action cannot relent, for it is at about this time that the schismatic tendencies referred to ripen."

The ideology of positive action is socialism. And in a liberated colonial territory socialism must set out consciously to grapple with certain issues "if independence is not to be alienated from the people." These issues are:

(1) To seek a connection with the egalitarian and humanist past of the people before their social evolution was ravaged by colonialism;

(2) To seek from colonialism those elements like new methods of industrial production and economic organization which can be adapted to serve the interests of the people;

(3) To seek ways and means of crushing the growth of class inequalities and antagonisms cre-

ated by the capitalist habit of colonialism;
(4) To reclaim the psychology of the people by erasing "colonial mentality";
(5) To defend the independence and security of the people.

As proof of its general validity, philosophical consciencism reduces its cardinal concepts into mathematic formulae. These are contained in the last chapter of the book.

There are a few ideological issues currently of worldwide significance on which philosophical consciencism has something clear-cut to say.

First, coexistence. Admitting that competing ideologies can be found in the same society and in different societies, consciencism holds that "while societies with different social systems can coexist, their ideologies cannot." It goes on: "There is such a thing as peaceful coexistence between states with different systems; but as long as oppressive classes exist, there can be no such thing as peaceful coexistence between opposing ideologies."

As a corollary of this view, philosophical consciencism holds that the end of imperialism is certain. But it adds that an end of imperialism "can only come about under pressure of nationalist awakening and an alliance of progressive forces which hasten its end and destroy its condition of existence."

Secondly, on socialism and revolution, philosophical consciencism is equally unequivocal. "Revolution is an indispensable avenue to socialism, where the antecedent social-political structure is animated by principles which are a negation of socialism, as in a capitalist structure (and therefore also in a colonialist structure, for a colonial structure is essentially ancillary to capitalism).... But from the ancestral line of communalism, the passage to socialism lies in reform, because the underlying principles are the same." Thus in relation to traditional African society, originally communalistic but largely ravaged by colonialism, socialism is historically revolutionary but genetically evolutionary.

Thirdly, the one-party state. Discussing a nation emerging from colonialism, philosophical consciencism holds that "a people's parliamentary democracy with a one-party system is better able to express and satisfy the common aspirations of a nation as a whole, than a multi-party parliamentary system, which is in fact only a ruse for perpetuating, and covers up, the inherent struggle between the 'haves' and the 'have-nots'."

Consciencism: Philosophy and Ideology for Decolonisation and Development has made its appearance at a very opportune moment when serious moves are being made in the direction of African unity.

It will provide the rallying ground for all sincere African patriots who feel that socialist ideology should more closely reflect the African background.

It will give the much-needed cue to many who talk of Nkrumaism but fail to define it in rational philosophical terms. And now that Nkrumaism has been authoritatively defined as the ideology of the New Africa, philosophical consciencism becomes the theoretical basis of Nkrumaism.

Above all, philosophical consciencism raises the problem of philosophy and ideology in Africa out of the quagmire of stagnation onto a higher plane of dynamic cohesion. Instead of an ideological standstill which maintains the intellectual strife in African society between the conflicting ideologies of traditional Africa, Islamic Africa and Euro-Christian Africa; instead of the vulgar and often irrational attempts to create brands of socialism (African, Arab, etc.) which leave Africa divided this time on a regional and linguistic basis; philosophical consciencism has created a system of thought which is a dialectical synthesis of all the dominant trends in African intellectual life. And because it achieves such a synthesis, philosophical consciencism will serve as the solid theoretical foundation on which a truly unifying ideology for all Africa can be built.

It is no surprise that Kwame Nkrumah, the leading architect and apostle of African unity, should also bring into being a systematized theoretical basis on which such an all-embracing unity could be founded and made to thrive.

PART TWO

Introduction

After the reactionary coup d'etat in Ghana on February 24, 1966, Nkrumah carried on the socialist revolutionary struggle from Guinea. He arrived in Conakry on March 2, 1966 and was at once proclaimed co-President of Guinea by President Sékou Touré and the Guinean Democratic Party (PDG).

Between March 1966 and August 1971, when Nkrumah left Conakry for medical treatment in Bucarest, the following books and pamphlets were published:

Books
  Challenge of the Congo, 1966
  Axioms (Freedom Fighters'
    Edition), 1966

Voice from Conakry, 1967
Dark Days in Ghana, 1968
Handbook of Revolutionary Warfare, 1968
Consciencism (Revised edition), 1970
Class Struggle in Africa, 1970
Revolutionary Path, (Published posthumously in 1973)

Pamphlets

The Spectre of Black Power
Ghana: The Way Out
The Big Lie
Two Myths
The Struggle Continues
} Written between 1966 and 1968

The full texts of these pamphlets were published in a single paperback in 1973 under the title *The Struggle Continues*.

In addition, Nkrumah worked on a book on the settler problem in Africa, with particular reference to Rhodesia. The title was to have been *Rhodesia: A case study of settler politics*. Tragically, Nkrumah became seriously ill before the book could be written, and

INTRODUCTION

his publishers were left with the task of publishing his collection of papers under the title *Rhodesia File*.

The books by Nkrumah published during the Conakry period provide essential and invaluable material for the student of Nkrumaism. They show his political philosophy in the light of the changing revolutionary situation in Africa. It is Nkrumah's political thought, expressed in this important work accomplished in Conakry which forms the second part of this summary of some of the fundamental features of Nkrumaism.

CHAPTER SEVEN

Neocolonialism

> The essence of neocolonialism is that the state which is subject to it, is in theory independent, and has all the outward trappings of international sovereignty. In reality, its economic system and thus its political policy is directed from outside. (*Neocolonialism*, p. ix.)

In *Neocolonialism: The last stage of imperialism*, first published in 1965, Nkrumah gave a detailed analysis of the workings of international monopoly capitalism in Africa, and showed how meaningless political freedom could be without economic independence. It is "sham independence".

Nkrumah considered neocolonialism to be more insidious, complex and dangerous than colonialism. "It not only prevents its victims from developing their economic potential for their own use, but it controls the political life of the country, and supports the indigenous bourgeoisie in perpetuating the oppression and exploitation of the masses. Under neocolonialism, the economic systems and political policies of independent territories are managed and manipulated from outside, by international monopoly finance capital in league with the indigenous bourgeoisie." (*Revolutionary Path*, p. 313.)

While political independence must be obtained before there can be fundamental economic and social change, the struggle to end all forms of exploitation takes place both before and after direct colonial rule ends. Within the national liberation movement are nationalist bourgeois elements which seek to end colonial rule but to preserve capitalist structures. During the campaign to win political freedom, differences between the various sectors forming the united anti-colonial front are blurred since the common objective to end colonialism binds all together. But once political independence has been won, fundamental differences between the long-term objectives of many of those forming the movement for national liberation result in splits and divisions which invariably occur along class lines.

The foundations of the neocolonialist or client state are laid during the period of the national liberation struggle. Nkrumah points out that the colonial power exploits differences between various sectors of the population "to orientate the leaders of the liberation movements to a brand of nationalism based on petty-minded and aggressive chauvinism as well as to steer the liberation movement along a reformist path. . . . Local agents, selected by the colonial power as 'worthy representatives' are then presented to the people as the champions of national independence, and are immediately given all the superficial attributes of power: a puppet government has been formed." (*Handbook*, pp. 9–10.)

The transition to neocolonialism involves the use of imperialist propaganda. Four examples are listed below:

(1) Western parliamentary democracy which arose out of the particular circumstances of European historical development is paraded as the ideal form of government for nations with quite different historical experiences.

(2) Capitalism, free enterprise and free competition is argued to be the only economic system capable of promoting development. The application of these capitalist doctrines has been largely responsible for the economic distortions and problems Africa can only overcome by the quite different processes of socialism.

(3) Policies of the Left invariably bring communism which is synonymous with totalitarian dictatorship. The great achievements of socialist countries are deliberately ignored.

(4) Cultural activities as long as they are backward-looking are fostered. These can encourage a sense of fatalism

and a concern with ethnic differences. The first can sap the will for political change; the second sanctifies the divisions among peoples and countries and can act as an obstacle in the way of efforts to end colonial balkanization.

If leaders of the national liberation struggle are vigilant, and possess genuinely revolutionary qualities "then and only then, does a truly independent government emerge, dedicated to national reconstruction in the liberated territory, and determined to assist all those engaged in anti-imperialist struggle." (*Ibid.*, p. 11.) In these circumstances, neocolonialists then resort to policies of encirclement and subversion in order to overthrow progressive governments using such weapons as "coup d'etats, assassination, mutiny within the party, tribal revolt, palace revolutions and so on, while at the same time strengthening neighbouring puppet regimes to form a political safety belt, a *cordon sanitaire.*" (*Ibid*, p. 11.)

Nkrumah considered neocolonialist

puppet governments even more insufferable than governments of territories still under direct colonial rule, "since they represent the exploitation and oppression of African by African." (*Revolutionary Path*, p. 59.) During the period of CPP government in Ghana, freedom fighters engaged in struggles to overthrow neocolonialist governments were given the same facilities to organize and to train as those fighting against colonial powers or settler minority governments.

Nkrumah described the mechanisms of neocolonialism as follows:

(1) Economic control in the form of "aid", "loans", trade and banking.
(2) The stranglehold of indigenous economies through vast interlocking multinational corporations with their subsidiaries and affiliates.
(3) Political direction through puppet governments.
(4) The cultivation of an indigenous bourgeoisie closely linked with the international bourgeoisie.

(5) The imposition of "defence" agreements, and the setting up of military, naval and air bases.

(6) Ideological propaganda through the mass communications media of press, radio and television – the emphasis being on anti-communism.

(7) The fomenting of discord between countries and tribes.

(8) Collective imperialism, such as the politico/military cooperation of the racist minority regimes of central and southern Africa.

(9) Activities of intelligence and espionage organizations and international agencies. The sending of "advisers" and "experts" (international bureaucrats), evangelists, Peace corps, etc.

In the words of Nkrumah; "The granting of economic 'aid' from capitalist countries is one of the most insidious ways in which neocolonialism hinders economic progress in the developing world, retarding industrialization and delaying the development of a large proletariat." (*Class Struggle*, p. 71.) While only a very small percentage of capitalist "aid" is spent on industrialization, aid from socialist countries is mainly spent on industrialization and the organization of profitable production. Aid from the socialist world is used for state projects; whereas "aid" from the west is almost entirely in the private sector.

"Invisible trade" channels, for example shipping, which is about 90 per cent controlled by capitalists, furnish imperialism with yet another means of economic penetration. In addition, the governments of so-called independent states help to strengthen and to perpetuate neocolonialism by bogus "nationalization" schemes which are often no more than participation agreements making the government collaborators with those who are exploiting Africa's human and material resources:

> They are combining with collective imperialism in the continuing exploitation of African workers and rural proletariat. The

African government shields the corporations from the resistance of the working class, and bans strikes or becomes the strike-breaker; while the corporations strengthen their stranglehold of the African economy, secure in the knowledge that they have government protection. In fact, the African governments become the policemen of imperialist, multinational corporations. There thus develops a common front to halt socialist advance. (*Ibid.*, p. 63.)

Similarly, African governments which form regional economic groupings are assisting in the continued oppression of the workers and peasants of Africa. For these regional organizations between governments which allow neocolonialism to operate in their midst, are obstacles in the advance of the African Revolution. They support neocolonialist controlled corporations and enterprises by enlarging their areas of operation, and by smoothing currency and tariff regulations.

Most of the African states are economically unviable, and are restricted within the artificial frontiers of colonialism. They are easy prey to neo-colonialist empire builders. "Where political balkanization has not been successful for the imperialists, economic balkanization has been pursued. A single productive process is divided between states.' (*Revolutionary Path*, p. 313.)

A relatively recent tactic of neo-colonialists is to appear to support liberation movements, or sections of liberation movements which are bourgeois nationalist and therefore do not aspire to socialist revolution:

> For the ending of direct colonial rule and the emergence of a puppet government facilitates neocolonialism by opening the door to exploitation from a wider range of neocolonialists than those represented by a single former colonial power. By concentrating political struggles to end direct colonial rule, or to force minority regimes to grant reforms, attention is diverted from economic and domestic issues, and the insidious processes of neocolonialism can proceed. Meanwhile, many of the puppet rulers of Africa masquerade as "revolutionaries" and "liberators", and serve the interest of their neocolonialist

masters by trying to mask the reactionary nature of their regimes. (*Ibid.*, pp. 313–14.)

While never for a moment underestimating the strength of neocolonialism, Nkrumah maintained that it represents the final stage of imperialism and indicates its weakness, since it implies the ineffectiveness of traditional methods of domination. He is confident that neocolonialism can and will be defeated, and sees the solution in a political programme which will bring about the total liberation of Africa and the formation of a socialist All-African Union Government:

> The immense resources of Africa can only be fully utilized to raise the standard of living of the masses if our continent is totally liberated from all forms of oppression and exploitation, and if our economy is developed on a continental basis. The essential pre-requisite is socialist planning within the framework of political unification. (*Ibid.*, p. 519.)

Nkrumah was convinced that all methods of struggle, including armed struggle, are necessary to complete the processes of the African Revolution.

Freedom is not freely given; it is won as a result of organized, sustained and irresistible pressure on the part of the oppressed. Neocolonialism, therefore, and all other forms of oppression can be banished from Africa through mass ideological education and training, and through unified political and military organization in solidarity with world socialist revolutionary forces.

CHAPTER EIGHT

Class struggle and the armed phase of the African Revolution

In the Author's Note to the revised edition of *Consciencism*, published in 1969, Nkrumah wrote:

> The issues are now clearer than they have ever been. The succession of military coups which have in recent years taken place in Africa, have exposed the close links between the interests of neocolonialism and the indigenous bourgeoisie. These coups have brought into sharp relief the nature and extent of the class struggle in Africa. Foreign monopoly capitalists are in close association with local reactionaries, and have made use of officers among the armed forces and police in order to frustrate the purposes of the African Revolution.

The changes made by Nkrumah in *Consciencism* occur principally in

Society and Ideology (Chap. 3), and mainly relate to his view of traditional African society and its relation to socialism and communism. While many African societies retain traces of a past which included the social practice of communalistic values, Nkrumah does not choose to pretend that pre-colonial African society was organized solely on that attractive basis. The truth of that period was both more complex and less ideal. Nkrumah appreciates the positive features of Africa's socio-political heritage, and the reflection of communalism in the emerging socialist Africa. However, he sees that theories which argue that Africa's communalist past means that socialism can be achieved without revolution are either naive or intended to help preserve the status quo.

Nkrumah rejects the myths and distortions of bourgeois historians who have maintained that Africa lies outside the mainstream of world historical development, and that class structures which exist in other parts of the world do not exist in Africa. "The African Revolution is an integral part of the world socialist revolution, and just as the class struggle is basic to world revolutionary processes, so also is it fundamental to the struggle of the workers and peasants of Africa." (*Class Struggle*, p. 10.)

The revisions to *Consciencism* were made shortly after Nkrumah had finished writing *Dark Days in Ghana*, his analysis of the pressures and processes resulting in the February 1966 coup in Ghana, and its effects on the African Revolution. In this book he examines the role of those sectors of the population which have close links with the international bourgeoisie, namely, those working in the state machinery, members of the western-oriented professional classes, officers of the armed forces and police trained in western academies, dishonest intellectuals, feudalists, sections of the petty bourgeoisie of town and country, the "small, selfish, money-minded, reactionary minority among vast masses of exploited and oppressed people." (*Class Struggle*, p. 12.) This minority, small but powerful because it is supported by imperialists and neocolonialists, is committed to capitalism and therefore to the continuance of privilege with all the suffering and injustice this entails for the ordinary people.

Nkrumah refers to the African bourgeoisie as the "internal" enemy of the African Revolution, and to imperialists and neocolonialists as the "external". "When the indigenous bourgeoisie and imperialism and neocolonialism are defeated, both the internal and the external enemies of the African Revolution will have been overcome, and the aspirations of the African people fulfilled." (*Ibid.*, p. 85.)

Ultimate victory for the people of Africa rests on "the ability of the socialist revolutionary party to assess the class position in society, and to see which classes and groups are for, and which against the revolution. The party must be able to mobilize and direct the vast forces for socialist revolution already existing, and to awaken and stimulate the immense revolutionary potential which is at present lying dormant." (*Ibid.*, p. 85.) Nkrumah concludes that there are only two ways of development open to an independent African state: "Either it must remain under imperialist domination via capitalism or neocolonialism; or it must pursue a socialist path by adopting the principles of scientific socialism." (*Ibid.*, p. 84.) In a neocolonialist situation there is no halfway to socialism.

To those who maintain that Africa is not ripe for socialist revolution since it does not have a sufficiently large and developed proletariat, Nkrumah points to the experience of peoples who have successfully achieved a fundamental transformation of society through a worker-peasant alliance. A relatively small proletariat if highly organized within a vanguard party committed to the principles of scientific socialism can take the revolution to the countryside. The peasantry, when politicized, then becomes with the urban and rural proletariat an integral part of the socialist revolutionary struggle. "The countryside is the bastion of the revolution. It is the revolutionary battlefield in which the peasantry in alliance with their natural class allies – proletariat and revolutionary intelligentsia – are the driving force for socialist construction and transformation." (*Ibid.*, p. 79.)

While Nkrumah recognized the emergence of a racial factor in the revolutionary struggle particularly in Africa, Asia and Latin America, he exposes it as reactionary and serving the interests of the international bourgeoisie by confusing and obscuring "the fundamental issue of socialist revolution which is the class struggle." (*Ibid.*, p. 83.) He regards the concept of the "Third World" as "neither a practical political concept nor a reality ... I do not deny the existence of the struggling 'wretched of the earth', but maintain they do not exist in isolation, as the 'Third World'. They are an integral part of the revolutionary world and are committed to the hilt in the struggle against capitalism to end the exploitation of man by man." (*The Myth of the "Third World"*, in *The Struggle Continues*, pp. 76–77.) Policies of non-alignment and co-existence applicable during the early nineteen sixties can no longer be upheld in the present world situation with the armed phase of the revolutionary struggle well-launched in Africa, Asia and Latin America:

> The world struggle, and the cause of world tension, has to be seen not in the old political context of the cold war, that is, of nation states and power blocs, but in terms of revolutionary and counter-revolutionary peoples. It cuts right across territorial boundaries and has nothing to to with colour or race. It is a war to the finish between the oppressed and the oppressors, between those who pursue a capitalist path, and those committed to socialist policies. (*Ibid.*, p. 76.)

When Nkrumah wrote of armed struggle and the tactics of violence and non-violence, he applies the terms in the modern revolutionary context. For example, "When a peasant in Africa or elsewhere dies of starvation in a world of plenty, they call it violence. It is violence when a whole class of people suffers indignity, deprivation and exploitation at the hands of a selfish, privileged minority. Reactionary violence must be met with revolutionary violence. The latter is employed every time the oppressed take action to end their oppression." (*Revolutionary Path*, p. 87.)

One of the most obvious forms of reactionary violence in recent times has been the military coup to oust a progressive government. Although the leaders of reactionary coups invariably proclaim that they are non-political and act to save the country from "economic chaos" and dishonest politicians, they are in fact the agents of imperialism and its internal allies, the indigenous bourgeoisie. They "reflect class interests and are part of the class struggle between capitalist and socialist revolution." (*Class Struggle*, p. 47.)

But the succession of reactionary military coups throughout the world indicates not the strength of the international bourgeoisie but its desperation and weakness. For they signify "the last ditch stand by indigenous exploiting classes and neocolonialists to preserve the bourgeois reactionary status quo". (*Ibid.*, p. 47.) In the case of revolutionary nationalist coups, these are carried out to end foreign politico-economic dominance, and are in the interests mainly of the nationalist bourgeoisie. In most cases, the position of workers and peasants are scarcely affected. "They continue to be exploited and oppressed, this time by the indigenous bourgeoisie with foreign business interests more concealed than ever behind a façade of nationalization policies." (*Ibid.*, p. 48.)

Then there are the coups which arise from power struggles within the bourgeois elites. These also reveal on the one hand the pressures of imperialism and neocolonialism, and on the other the growing strength of the awakening

African masses driving the local bourgeoisie and their neocolonialist masters to increasingly extreme and violent measures to protect their privileged positions.

As Nkrumah said in his last sessional address to the Ghana National Assembly on 1st February, 1966: "It is not the duty of the army to rule or govern, because it has no political mandate and its duty is not to seek a political mandate. . . . If the national interest compels the armed forces to intervene then immediately after the intervention the army must hand over to a new civil government elected by the people and enjoying the people's mandate under a constitution accepted by them. . . . The substitute of a military regime or dictatorship is no solution to the neocolonialist problem." (*Revolutionary Path*, pp. 370–1.)

On the question of the one party system of government often given as the excuse for overturning a progressive government by force, Nkrumah maintains one party rule to be a safe and efficient instrument for serving the people if it operates "within the framework of a socialist state or in a developing state with a socialist programme. The government governs through the people, and not through class cleavages and interests. In other words, the basis of government is the will of the people." (*Ibid.*, p. 373.) On the other hand, a one party government in a neocolonialist client state can "quickly develop into the most dangerous form of tyranny, despotism and oppression." (*Ibid.*, p. 372.)

With Nkrumah, theory and practice went side by side. For example, having assessed the puppet state and revealed its class basis and close links with international finance capital, he puts forward practical solutions recognizing that all forms of struggle, including armed struggle, must be employed. For neocolonialism functioning through the puppet states can only be overthrown by force. Preparations, therefore, must be made for the people's armed struggle as the highest form of political action. This is not to be merely an armed struggle, but a revolution organized under the leadership of a vanguard party committed to scientific socialism.

In the *Handbook of Revolutionary Warfare*, dedicated "To the African guerrilla", Nkrumah outlines the political and military organization which could, through unified all-African strategy and tactics, bring victory in the armed phase of the African Revolution. It may be summarized as:

1. The formation of an All-African People's Revolutionary Party (AAPRP) to co-ordinate policies and to direct action.
2. The creation of an All-African People's Revolutionary Army (AAPRA) to unify our liberation forces and to carry the armed struggle through to final victory.
(*Handbook*, p. 56.)

Controlling **AAPRP** and **AAPRA** would be the All-African Committee for Political Co-ordination (AACPC). This organization would link all liberated territories and progressive parties under a common ideology, and would provide "an organic link with the peoples of Africa, Asia and Latin America who are struggling against imperialism; ensure permanent relations with the socialist states of the world; maintain and create links with all workers' movements in the capitalist-imperialist states." (*Ibid.*, pp. 57–8.) The triple chain of command of AAPRA stemming from the supreme AACPC involves close co-ordination between conventional and guerrilla units at all levels, and between political and military wings of the combined AACPC–AAPRA organization. The armed forces would always be subordinate to, and under the control of the political leadership. Eventually, as the people's revolutionary struggle progressed, professional armies would be phased out, until with the formation of a Union Government they would disappear completely and the defence of Africa would rest on a continental people's militia.

Nkrumah always thought in terms of the African continent as a whole within the context of the world socialist revolutionary struggle. The total liberation and unification of Africa and the formation of a socialist All-African Union Government are the essential processes through which the people of Africa can be truly liberated and free to develop their human and material resources for their own needs.

CHAPTER NINE

Socialist All-African Union Government

> At the core of the concept of African unity lies socialism and the socialist definition of the New African society.
> Socialism and African unity are organically complementary. (*Handbook*, p. 28.)

In 1963, the same year as *Africa Must Unite* was published, the Organization of African Unity (OAU) was founded largely as a result of Nkrumah's initiative. He thought at that time that the political unification of Africa might be achieved by the voluntary action of independent African governments. But although Article Two of the Charter declared that the first purpose of the OAU was to promote the unity and solidarity of the African states, it was "a Charter of *intent* rather than a Charter of positive action.... The nature of the embryonic institutions provided for in the Charter, and the lack of provision for an All-African High Command to give teeth to the Organization meant that the OAU suffered from the start from inherent weaknesses." (*Revolutionary Path*, pp. 249–50.)

Between 1963 and 1965, Nkrumah strongly urged the immediate setting up of unified political, economic and military machinery, however embryonic, as first steps in the practical process of total liberation and unification. But those who supported a gradualist approach, preferring to concentrate on economic and cultural co-operation, and on regional economic groupings, persistently blocked his attempts to achieve even the most rudimentary political unity.

In 1965, at the Accra Summit meeting of the OAU, Nkrumah made what was to be his final call for the setting up of an Executive Council and an All-African High Command. The Summit was held when the Unilateral Declaration of Independence in Rhodesia (UDI), was imminent. Yet as so often in past crises, the OAU failed to act. There followed UDI, a succession of reactionary military coups, and a general stepping up of imperialist and neocolonialist aggression throughout Africa. "While the independent African states hang so tenaciously to their separate identities and interests, the enemies of the African people, the imperialists and neocolonialists and their local agents, strengthen the bonds which unite them, and set us an example in planning on a continental scale." (*Revolutionary Path*, p. 368.)

In the books he wrote in Conakry, Nkrumah reviews the record of the OAU and comes to the conclusion that "as it is now constituted, the OAU is not likely to be able to achieve the political unification of Africa." (*Handbook*, p. 41.) Like the United Nations Organization (UNO), and indeed any other political organization, the OAU can only be as effective as its members wish it to be. The presence of neo-colonialist governments within the OAU, although paying lip service to Article Two of the Charter, in fact guarantee its non-implementation.

Nkrumah had become convinced that total liberation and unification must be achieved through the direct action of the people of Africa expressed through continental political organization and armed force. Basic to both is class struggle. He saw the African continent not in terms of numbers of independent states but as a continent divided into combat zones. There are:

(1) Liberated areas
(2) Zones under enemy control
(3) Contested areas

He defines liberated areas as zones in which "a social revolution is taking place to consolidate independence." (*Handbook*, p. 44.) Although with the possible exceptions of areas administered by freedom fighter movements, no "liberated areas" can be said to "come fully up to all the standards required of them . . . the main criterion for judging them to be liberated is the actual direction in which they are moving, since our assessment is of changing not static phenomena." (*Ibid.*, p. 46.)

Zones under enemy control are those controlled by imperialism:

(a) through an administration manned by foreigners. The territory is then externally subjected.
(b) through a puppet government made up of local elements. The territory is then both internally and externally subjected.
(c) through a settler minority government. In this territory, settlers have established the rule of a majority by a minority. There is no logic except the right of might which can accept such a situation. (*Ibid.*)

Contested zones are those territories in which the people have reached an advanced stage of revolutionary organization and are actively and strongly challenging the enemies of the African Revolution. "Between a zone under enemy control where the masses are awakening and a hotly-contested zone, there is only one missing link: a handful of genuine revolutionaries prepared to organize and to act." (*Ibid.*, p. 49.)

Nkrumah suggested practical measures which might be taken, emphasizing the class content of the struggle, and charting the kind of continental politico/military machinery required. This is summed up in the AAPRP–AAPRA structure defined in the *Handbook*, involving the formation of an All-African People's Revolutionary Party and an All-African People's Revolutionary Army consisting of both guerrilla and conventional forces, under the control of an All-African Committee for Political Co-ordination (AACPC). The Central Committee of the Party might then develop to become the *de facto* governing body of a united Africa.

Nkrumah, in stressing the role of armed force in the African Revolution, did not rule out non-violent methods. These have their place in all revolutionary struggle, the realities of a situation being the factors determining the most effective strategy and tactics to be employed at a particular time and place. But he considered that "revolutionary warfare is the logical, inevitable answer to the political, economic and social situation in Africa today. We do not have the luxury of an alternative. We are faced with a necessity." (*Handbook*, p. 42.)

African revolutionary forces are confronted with the task of eliminating both the internal and the external enemies of the African people. Remnants of colonialism must be destroyed; racist minority regimes overthrown; and neocolonialist puppet governments replaced by those truly representative of the people. For contrary to the much recommended view that there must be no interference in the internal affairs of states, Nkrumah held it to be the positive duty of those in a position to do so, to interfere in "enemy-held" areas.

What is required is the full mobilization of Africa's human resources for a people's war. This will take the form of protracted guerrilla warfare involving the entire population, and at the same time the adoption of such non-violent methods of struggle as boycotts, strikes, non-cooperation and so on. "For although the African nation is at present split up among separate states, it is in reality simply divided into two: our enemy and ourselves." (*Ibid.*, p. 48.) In brief, the "enemy" is the international bourgeoisie and its local agents; "ourselves" implies all progressive people striving towards a just society.

The ultimate objective of Nkrumah's policies remained: "a unified socialist society in which the African Personality will find full expression." (*Revolutionary Path*, p. 520.) This implies the total liberation and unification of Africa, and socialist development and utilization of the vast material and human resources of the continent. For it is only through unification and socialism that Africa's economic problems can be solved.

Economic size, or the "optimum zone of development" is essential for an integrated modern economy. The optimum zone of development for the African people is the entire African continent. In the words of Nkrumah: "Africa is one: this battle must be fought and won continentally." (*Handbook*, p. 43.) Africa, with a socialist All-African Union Government, and with a people politicized through ideological training and revolutionary experience, would then become a positive and strong bulwark of the socialist world.

Nkrumah's final message to the people of Africa is expressed in the Conclusion to his last book. *Revolutionary Path*, which ends as follows:

> The African people, in solidarity with comrades in every part of the world, have the means, the ability and the determination to banish once and for all, imperialism, neocolonialism, settler minority rule, and all forms of oppression from our continent. A unified and socialist society in which the African Personality will find full expression can and must be constructed. There is victory for us.

Bucarest
15 October 1972

www.ingramcontent.com/pod-product-compliance
Lightning Source LLC
Chambersburg PA
CBHW021127300426
44113CB00006B/329